KRILOF AND HIS FABLES

KRILOF AND HIS FABLES

By W. R. S. RALSTON, M.A.
Of the British Museum . .

STRAHAN AND CO. PUBLISHERS
56 LUDGATE HILL, LONDON
1869

DALZIEL BROTHERS
Camden Press
ENGRAVERS & PRINTERS

Тѣхъ русскихъ, которымъ попадется этотъ переводъ уважаемаго баснописца, переводчикъ покорнѣйше проситъ принять въ соображеніе, что иллюстрированіе книги нисколько отъ него не зависѣло.

PREFACE.

THE poems of which a literal prose translation is now
offered to the English reader enjoy a popularity in
their native land which they can scarcely expect to obtain in
a foreign country. At home they live on the lips and in the
memories of old and young, of rich and poor, and have become a sort of national heirloom; abroad they run the risk
of being regarded as little more than quaint curiosities.
Much of their special excellence depends upon the choice
felicity of their language and the artistic structure of their
verse; it is, therefore, scarcely possible for any one to form
a fair idea of their original merits who makes their acquaintance only after they have been interpreted into alien prose.
But, even in a foreign dress, I think that they cannot fail to
interest and to please such readers as will make fair allow-
ance for the disadvantages under which they labour. Their
brilliance has naturally been dimmed, and their music has

been altogether stilled; but their shrewd insight into the thoughts and motives of the human heart, their ingenious interpretation of the inarticulate sentiments which prevail in the world of brutes, and their faculty of relating a story clearly and concisely, all these remain; and all these can be appreciated by the foreign reader. The pictures of Russian life, also, which their words offer are perfectly intelligible to all who take the trouble to study them, and will convey to a stranger's mind a far more correct idea of Russian manners and customs than he can gain from the cleverest illustrations which fancy can suggest to an artist whose knowledge of the subject is imperfect. In the stories, for instance, of "The Two Peasants," "The Peasant in Trouble," "The Three Moujiks," "The Peasant and the Labourer," and several others of the same class, a store of information will be found respecting the sayings and doings of the common people of Russia, those many millions of fellow-Europeans of whom we know much less than we do of the Chinese or the American Indians. Still more interesting should be the protests which some of them offer against the oppression and corruption which so long prevailed in Russia; against the manner in which the strong trod down the weak, and the rich ground the faces of the poor. It is pleasant to mark the generous sympathy with wronged weakness, the hardy indignation against guilty strength, which prompted Krilof to pen such apologues as those of "The Peasants and the River," "The Bear among the Bees," and "The Dancing Fish." Such stories as these can never be entirely divested of their attraction, even when they have been stripped of their ornaments and clothed in an unaccustomed and prosaic garb.

Most of the translators of these fables have tried to turn them into verse.*   I have not ventured to attempt a similar task, but have confined my efforts to the production of what I hope is a faithful prose rendering of Krilof's poetry. The version may be disfigured by the ungainliness of a photographic portrait, but it aims at possessing something of a photograph's fidelity. The only liberty I have allowed myself with the fables I have selected for translation has been sometimes to omit the "moral" when it did not seem indispensable. Krilof is never tedious as a moralist, but all "morals" and "applications," and such-like tags and commentaries, are apt to become tiresome. I should not be surprised if the notes which I have myself added bore witness to the truth of this assertion.

I have translated about half of the entire collection of Krilof's fables. Of those I have omitted, a considerable part is composed of the imitations with which Krilof commenced his career as a fabulist, and of which I have thought it sufficient to give a couple of specimens. The rest are chiefly pieces which seem less original and characteristic than those I have selected, or which appear comparatively pointless now, though they had a special interest at the time they were written, and for the readers for whom they were intended.

---

* One of the exceptions is Mr. Sutherland Edwards, who has given prose renderings of most of the fables he has inserted in his excellent article on Krilof. It is to be found in his " Russians at Home "—by far the best English book about Russia.

It should be borne in mind that Krilof's fables were seldom mere literary bubbles, blown to create an instant's amusement or admiration, but not intended to serve any useful end, or to suggest any serious idea. Each of them, as a general rule, conveyed either a valuable warning or a wholesome repfimand.

Before bringing this preface to a close, I wish to acknowledge my obligations to the several writers from whom I have borrowed. For some reason which I cannot clearly explain, English translators from the Russian have shown a singular unwillingness to refer to the predecessors who have made their task comparatively easy. It has been a common practice to make copious, if not exclusive, use of a French or German translation of a Russian work, and then utterly to ignore the obligation. This course of behaviour appears to me injudicious, being apt to expose those who follow it to unpleasant comments. I think that, in translating from so unfamiliar a language as the Russian, one should by all means make use of such assistance as preceding translators. have to offer; but let that assistance be frankly acknowledged.

In my own case, although my translations have been made from the original Russian, yet I have to express my thanks to M. Charles Parfait* for his spirited translation of the fables into French verse, and to M. Ferdinand Torney†

---

* " Fables de Krilof, traduites en vers français par Charles Parfait." Paris (H. Plon), 1867. 8vo.

† " Iwan Krylow's Fabeln. Aus dem Russischen von Ferdinand Torney." Mitau und Leipzig, 1842. 8vo.

and an anonymous German lady* for their versions into German verse—versions which are singularly faithful, considering the difficulties with which they have had to contend. For the sketch of Krilof's life I am almost entirely indebted to the memoirs written (in Russian) by M. Pletnef, by M. Lobanof, and by M. Grot, of the Academy of Sciences of St. Petersburg.

I gladly seize this opportunity of expressing my thanks to M. Grot for many kindnesses, and, among others, for his gift of the excellent and thoroughly exhaustive critique by M. Kenevich,† from which I have drawn most of the notes which I have inserted (between brackets) at the end of some of the fables.

Lastly, I have to thank another Russian friend, M. Alexander Onegine, for the trouble he has taken in revising my translation, thereby securing me against that dread of possible blunders innocently committed, which so often hangs like a dreary shadow about a translator's seldom overenviable path.

W. R. S. R.

Inner Temple,
   Dec. 14, 1868.

---

* "Fabeln von Krylow, treu übersetzt aus dem Russischen ins Deutsche, von einer Deutschen." St. Petersburg, 1863. 8vo.

† "Bibliograficheskiya i istoricheskiya primyechania k basnyam Kruilova. Sostavil V. Kenevich." Sanktpeterburg, 1868. 4to.

CONTENTS.

CONTENTS.

MEMOIR.

—o—

RATHER more than a hundred years ago,* a boy was born at Moscow, on whom Fortune seemed at first by no means disposed to smile, but who was destined to enjoy in after-life a singular amount of honour and success. His father, a captain in the infantry of the line, found his income scarcely sufficient for the support of even a small family, and had no reason for hoping that the future would bring him better times.

Soon after the birth of the little Ivan Andreëvich, the captain's family followed his regiment into the east of Russia; and, after a time, found themselves at Orenburg, in the midst of the troubles caused by the insurrection of Pugachef, the insurgent leader, who produced so great a disturbance by giving himself out to be the Emperor Peter III. That unfortunate monarch had in reality been assassinated several years before; but a story had got abroad that he had managed to escape from death, and was living somewhere in concealment; so

---

* On February $\frac{2}{14}$, 1768, according to general report; but some writers think he was born a few years earlier.

b

the minds of many men were prepared to accept Pugachef's daring statement. Accordingly, the impostor soon raised a numerous army, and for some time set the imperial troops at defiance.

During the period of his success, he attacked the fortress in which the elder Krilof was stationed, and was so enraged at the obstinacy with which it was defended, that he declared he would hang that officer and all the members of his family. They all ultimately contrived to escape; but tradition states that they were often in great danger, and that on one occasion, when they were halting in a village post-house, the little Ivan was hidden out of harm's way in a large piece of earthenware which stood in the cottage.

From Orenburg, they went to Tver; and there the captain, finding that his expenses were becoming greater than his income, retired from the army, and obtained a post in the civil service. A few years later, he died, leaving very little to his son, now a lad of fourteen, beyond a large box of books, which had followed him in all his wanderings.

After a time, the boy obtained employment in the public service, but of so unremunerative a nature that his mother determined to go with him to St. Petersburg, in hopes of obtaining a pension there as an officer's widow. All that she did obtain was a post for her son, with the salary of two roubles (about six shillings) a month.* He remained in

---

* Money went further then, of course, than it will now. For instance, the wages paid to the servant kept by Madame Krilof were two roubles a year only. Still the little household must have been often reduced to great straits.

the public service till the year 1788, when he lost his mother.

She has been described as "a simple-minded woman, who had received scarcely any education," but one of great worth and of considerable strength of character. She had done her best to obtain a good education for her boy, reading Russian with him herself, and making him, when he was studying French, read all his translations aloud to her— although she did not understand a word of the language from which they were rendered. By means of little presents and rewards, she induced him to study hard, and he soon took very kindly to books. The old volumes which had formed his father's travelling library he read over and over again with delight, and, from the perusal of the histories which were among them, his mind became full of ideas about classic Greece and ancient Russia. Vague ideas concerning the stage next began to float through his head, and, after a time, they shaped themselves into a drama, called the "Cofeinitsa,"* which he wrote (if the date of his birth may be trusted) before he was sixteen years old. This he offered to a bookseller, who gave him sixty paper roubles for it (about as many francs), or rather, at Krilof's express desire, books to that amount. The works he chose were those of Racine, Boileau, and Molière, preferring them to those of Voltaire and Crébillon. Years afterwards, when he had become famous, the bookseller gave him back the MS., which he

---

* A "Cofeinitsa" is a fortune-teller who looks for auguries in coffee-grounds.

had never published, and the poet re-read it with a pleasure not altogether free from regret.

The lad next turned his attention to tragedy, and produced a piece called " Cleopatra," which he showed to his friend, the celebrated actor, Dmitrievsky. The actor went carefully over it with him, and pointed out so many faults that Krilof gave it up in despair, and began another, under the title of " Philomela." This also, which was finished in 1786, and was printed nine years later in the collection of Russian dramas published by the Academy of Sciences, failed to meet with the actor's approval. So the young author gave up the drama for a time.

After the death of his mother, which took place when he was twenty years old, Krilof found himself entirely alone in the world, and free to occupy himself as he pleased. So he soon gave up his employment in the public service, and determined to devote himself to literature.

In partnership with a retired officer of literary tastes, who had a printing establishment of his own, he founded a journal, or rather a monthly satirical magazine, called the " Spirit-Post ;"* but, cleverly as it was written, it was not a commercial success, and, after a year, it stopped. By this time, Krilof had become the sole proprietor of the printing-press, which occupied a room in the house which then stood where the Oldenburg Palace stands now, close to the Summer Garden. Then he began to print a new journal, called the "Spectator,"†

---

* *Pochta Dukhof.*   † *Zritel.*

which lasted eleven months. Those were bad days for journalists in Russia, and the circulation of the "Spectator" did not exceed 170 copies.* As soon as it had run its brief course, Krilof started a third journal, under the title of the "St. Petersburg Mercury;" but, after a year's existence, this also came to a close, never having secured more than 150 subscribers. After its demise, Krilof discontinued his own publications, but he continued to print for others.

By this time, he had become well known in the world of letters, and, as he was also a good musician and an agreeable companion, he was much sought after in society. Most of his biographers relate that he led a jovial and careless life until 1801, when the Empress Maria Fedorovna obtained a post for him at Riga, under Prince Sergius Galitsin.† But M. Grot, of the Academy of Sciences, points out that this is a mistake. Krilof had, long before that time, become intimate with the Prince, in whose house he lived for a while at Moscow, and whom he accompanied first into Lithuania, and then to his country house in the province of Saratof, in South-east Russia. There he remained till the year 1801.

This was an important period in his life, for it enabled him to study the country well, and the ways of the country people.

---

* At that time, Karamzin's "Moscow Journal," the periodical which then had the largest circulation, could boast of only 300 subscribers.

† There are many princes of this name in Russia ; so many, that tradition relates how a nobleman who, one day, attempted to pass over a river in a ferry-boat without payment, claiming exemption on the ground that he was a Prince Galitsin, was indignantly addressed by the ferryman with the words, "Am not I a Prince Galitsin too?" And so he really was.

When at Tver, in his boyish days, he was always fond of associating with the common folk, the "black people," as they are called in Russia; and he would spend whole hours in wandering about the bazaars or the places where the moujiks were amusing themselves, or in sitting on the banks of the Volga, listening to the conversation of the washer-women who congregated there, and gossiped over their work. While at Prince Galitsin's he had again an opportunity of mixing among the peasantry, and of making himself thoroughly acquainted with the joys and sorrows of village life. There he could see for himself how hard was too often the peasant's lot, how heavy was the pressure under which he had to groan. It was there, in all probability, that he stored up those impressions of the country to which he afterwards so often gave form and colour in his fables. There, too, he was able to study the curious scene presented by a rich noble's country house; for Prince Galitsin lived in great state, keeping up a band of forty musicians to play to him, and employing altogether as many as six hundred retainers in his household. The Prince and all his family were very kind to the young poet, who used to teach the children of the house, and get up little musical and theatrical entertainments for the amusement of his hosts. The only things he had to complain of were the gnats and flies, which are certainly very trying in Russia, and particularly in the neighbourhood of the Volga, and which he used to try to avoid by mounting to the top of the village belfry, where he was one day found, fast asleep among the bells.

When the Emperor Alexander I. mounted the throne, in 1801, he recalled Prince Galitsin from his retirement in the country, and made him military governor of Livonia. Krilof went with him as a secretary, but did not long act in that capacity; for it soon turned out that he had no great talent for business, and, besides that, he began to devote himself to gambling with what seemed likely to be a fatal passion. But he stayed with the Prince, as a friend and companion, till 1804, when his patron gave up his appointment, and then he returned to St. Petersburg. According to the usual accounts, it was then that he went to the Prince's estates in the province of Saratof; but it seems more likely that he took to leading a wandering life at that time, and continued it for some years, going from one Russian city to another, as fancy led him. He is said to have won a very large sum of money at cards during his residence in Riga, so that he could well afford to be idle and extravagant for a time.

What is certain is, that towards the end of the year 1805 he spent some time in Moscow, and became intimate with the literary celebrities of that capital. To one of these, the celebrated poet and fabulist Dmitrief, Krilof one day showed some fables which he had adapted from La Fontaine. Struck by their spirit and animation, Dmitrief inserted them in the " Moscow Spectator," where they obtained a decided success, and strongly recommended their author to cultivate this style of writing. Krilof's fame may be said to date from that epoch. He was nearly forty years old before he found out in what his strength lay.

In 1806 he returned to St. Petersburg, and soon afterwards obtained a Government appointment, which he held for some years. In 1807 he produced two comedies, which obtained considerable success on the stage. The one was called " The Fashions-Shop,"* and the other " A Lesson for Daughters,"† and both of them were levelled against that taste for everything French, which was always so excessively distasteful to Krilof. With their appearance his dramatic career came to a close, and thenceforward he was content to base his reputation on his fables, of which the first collection, twenty-three in number, was published in the year 1809; and the second, containing twenty-one more, in 1811. In 1812 he was appointed to a very congenial post in the Imperial Public Library, which had just been reorganized and placed under the direction of his intimate friend, Olenine. The officers to whom the various departments were entrusted were all men of learning and literary tastes, and the section of Russian Literature was confided to Sopikof, a very learned authority on Slavonic bibliography. Krilof entered the Library as his assistant, and, six years later, succeeded him in his post and in his official quarters. That position he continued to hold till the year 1841, when he definitively retired from the public service. Long before that time his fables had made him the most popular writer in Russia.

The years he spent in the Public Library, almost thirty in number, glided peacefully away. He was a man of but few

---

* *Modnaya Lavka.*   † *Urok Dochkam.*

wants, and such as he had he could easily satisfy. Besides his salary, he had a pension of at first about sixty pounds a year, and afterwards of twice that amount; so he was sufficiently well off. His position in the literary and scientific world was a very pleasant one. His fame as a popular author was continually increasing, his presence was greatly prized and sought after in society, and he was treated with almost affectionate kindness by the imperial family. He might, if he had liked, have revolved in the most distinguished circles; but his tastes were very simple, and he had little sympathy with gilded magnificence. His quarters in the Public Library suited him admirably, and so did his post, in which he had little to disturb him. The rooms which he had inherited from his predecessor, Sopikof, were on the second floor of the building, their windows looking out on the Gostinnoi-Dvor, the principal bazaar of St. Petersburg—a huge collection of shops, the arcades surrounding which are enlivened all day by the presence of crowds of loungers or intending purchasers. From his rooms Krilof could look down at his ease on the busy scene below, and could listen contentedly to the conversations which were constantly going on there between the merchants and their customers, or among the peasants and the droshky-drivers, who are accustomed to loiter in picturesque groups about the street which divides the Library from the bazaar. After his official labours were over for the day, he used to go to the English Club, so called because it was originally founded by an Englishman, and there he would dine heartily, and then enjoy a doze. For some time after his death, a certain stain, due to the pressure of his head during the nap which was his "usual custom of an afternoon," was carefully preserved upon the walls of the club. When his doze was over, he would sometimes go to the theatre; but more frequently he stayed where he was, playing cards till it was time to go home. As he grew older and more unwieldy, he went out more rarely into society; but there were a few houses which he always loved to frequent, especially that of the Olenines, by whom he was treated as if he had been a member of the family. In the literary, artistic, and scientific circles of St. Petersburg it has always been possible to enjoy the pleasures of society without encountering its drawbacks. The idea of giving parties "out of revenge" has never been able to naturalize itself there; and men of narrow means have not thought it necessary to hamper their mutual intercourse by restrictions borrowed from the code of opulent festivity. Consequently, Krilof was able to spend a sociable evening with his friends, whenever the idea occurred to him, without being compelled to submit to such changes of dress as would have sorely vexed him. For he was careless to a fault in his costume. At home, he generally wore an old and tattered dressing-gown, and he had a strong objection to renewing his wardrobe. When his old clothes were worn out, his friends used sometimes to get him invested in new ones by dint of stratagem; but it was impossible to instil into him the reverence with which such objects are generally regarded by well-regulated minds. Gloves he never would condescend to wear, even in the depth of winter. "I always lose them," he used to plead, "and my hands never get cold." And, indeed, his circulation was singularly vigorous. When he lived near the Summer Garden, he used to bathe every day in the adjacent canal, and he continued this practice even when the water was covered by a thin coat of ice. So great was his contempt for clothes that, in hot weather, he would sometimes dispense with all but his shirt; and on one occasion, when, thus simply clad, he was playing the violin, he was so carried away by the tide of musical feeling, that he spent some time tranquilly performing at his open window—quite unaware that he was presenting a singular spectacle to the world of fashion then promenading in the Summer Garden. He had an eccentric habit of appropriating any stray napkin or towel, or the like, that might be lying about a room, and of afterwards producing it from his pocket, under the impression that it was his hand-kerchief, and waving it before the eyes of the astonished company. Perhaps the strangest story told on good authority of his absence of mind in things sartorial is that of his going to court on one occasion in a new uniform. His friend Olenine, just before entering the presence-chamber, thought it as well to scrutinize Krilof's costume, and discovered that he had got on so new a coat, that its buttons were still enveloped in the silver paper which the tailor had carefully wrapped round them.

The state of his apartments was in keeping with that of his dress. Neither order nor cleanliness had charms for his eyes. Nothing was ever cleaned or put to rights in his rooms : his books lay about anywhere ; undisturbed dust accumulated upon everything.   He was very fond of birds ; and, twice a day, he used to strew his floor with oats, on which the pigeons, which haunted the adjacent bazaar— sacred birds to Russian eyes—would descend in flocks, finding easy access through the open window.

During one brief period, the rooms wore a totally different appearance ; but the change did not last long.   Krilof had sold a new edition of his fables for a large sum of money, and did not know what to do with it.   At first, he thought of spending it in travelling abroad ; but he soon gave up that idea.   Then he determined to expend it upon the embellishment of his apartments.   Upholsterers were called in ; sumptuous furniture was freely bought.   The floors were covered with costly carpets ; silken hangings adorned the walls and windows.   Choice pictures were hung up on all sides, flanked by mirrors in gleaming frames ; and, wherever an inch of standing-room could be found, there was placed a crystal vase, or a delicate statuette, or some fragile form of beauty in glass.   The whole abode seemed transformed as by the wave of a fairy's wand, and the owner might well be excused if he felt proud of the change he had produced, when the newly decorated rooms were lighted up on the occasion of the feast to which he invited his bosom friends in honour of his apartments' metamorphosis.

But he soon grew tired of all this unwonted splendour. A few days after the inaugural banquet, one of his friends happened to call upon him, and found that he had returned to his old ways. The rich carpets were strewn with oats, on which a greedy flock of pigeons was feeding. Every time the door opened, away flew the birds in a hurry, upsetting the crystals, overthrowing the statuettes, shivering the glass into fragments. A very short time sufficed to reduce the room to its normal state of dirt and disorder, from which it never recovered as long as Krilof occupied it. Only, before the ruin took place, a sketch of this sumptuous study was taken for the Grand Duchess Maria Nikolaevna, which still preserves the memory of the fabulist's short-lived magnificence.

As may well be supposed, his servants were none of the best. An old woman, assisted by her daughter, waited upon him, and took care not to trouble him by any excess of housewifely zeal. Nothing was ever cleaned; not a book was ever known to be dusted. If a visitor arrived, he did not know where to deposit his hat in safety, nor where to find a seat from which he could rise unsoiled. Krilof never troubled himself about such superfluities as a writing-desk or a cabinet. Even such necessaries as pens and ink and paper were seldom to be discovered without painful research.

One of his friends, in describing a visit which he paid the poet, states that he found him smoking a cigar, which kept going out. Each time it went out, he called the servant-girl in to give him a light; so at last she brought a candle without a candlestick, dropped a little melted tallow on the table, and stuck the candle in it for her master's convenience. He was greatly addicted to tobacco, we may take this opportunity of observing, and would often smoke, says Lobanof, "from thirty-five to fifty cigars a day." It is to be hoped that they were cigarettes or papirosses.

It was dangerous, as might be imagined, to lend Krilof a book of any value. On one occasion, he was sitting at breakfast, reading a large and valuable volume he had borrowed from his friend and patron, Olenine, when suddenly he overbalanced himself, and, in trying to avoid a fall, he upset the coffee-pot over the book. Rushing wildly into the kitchen, he carried off a bucket of water, and began to pour its contents over the book as it lay on the ground. Seeing this, his scared servant-maid burst into the rooms of his colleague, Gnedich, and horrified him by the news that her master had gone out of his mind.

This, by the way, was not the only occasion on which his eccentric demeanour savoured of madness to vulgar understandings. Once, it is said, when he was very young, he was stopping in the country with Count Tatischef, when his host was suddenly called away to town. The Count, whose whole family was to go with him, allowed Krilof, at his own request, to remain where he was. As soon as the young poet found himself alone, he began to carry out an idea he had long cherished, and to lead a life as similar as was possible to that led by man in unsophisticated times. With that view, he gave up devoting any time to his toilette, discontinued shaving, and allowed his hair and nails to grow as they liked. Books, however, he did not discard; but, instead of reading them at home, he spent the entire day over them in the garden. One day, as he was strolling there, presenting a strange and hermit-like appearance, the sound of wheels was suddenly heard, and, before he could escape into the house, the Count and all his family, returning unexpectedly, drove past the very spot where he was. Their surprise may be well conceived. His confusion was probably as great then as it was on the occasion of another misadventure which happened to him in early youth. When he was first at St. Petersburg, he used to spend a good deal of time at the house of his friend, the actor Dmitrievsky. It happened that at one time his visits were discontinued for a while, and during that interval Dmitrievsky changed his quarters. One day, Dmitrievsky met his young friend, and invited him to dinner. At the appointed hour Krilof, who knew nothing about the change of address, appeared at the wonted door. It was opened by a servant, who told him that her master was out. "I'll come in and wait for him," said Krilof, making his way into what had been his friend's bed-room, and there unceremoniously going to sleep on the bed. Now it happened that the rooms were then occupied by a Chinovnik and his wife. Presently they returned home, and the lady went straight to her room without having learned that a visitor had arrived during her absence. Her astonishment may be imagined when she discovered an utterly unknown young man tranquilly slumbering on the bed. The shriek which she naturally uttered on seeing the sleeping stranger called her husband to her side, and awoke the involuntary trespasser, who at first had some difficulty in accounting for his totally unexpected appearance there. It was certainly an awkward position to retire from gracefully.

To his next-door neighbour, Gnedich, he was greatly attached, heartily enjoying his society. Gnedich had translated the "Iliad," and was fond of holding forth on the subjects of Homer's merits and those of Greek writers in general. One day, Krilof, who was then fifty years old, talked about learning Greek. Gnedich told him he was too old, that no one could learn a new language after such and such an age, and added various other similar remarks of equal value. Krilof made no reply; but, the next day, he began to study Greek, making use of a New Testament in which the original was accompanied by a Slavonic translation, and being thus saved the trouble of consulting a dictionary. For two years he continued his studies in secret. At the end of that time, he happened to be present one day when Gnedich was complaining that he could not understand a certain passage in Homer. "I should read it this way," said Krilof, favouring him with an impromptu translation. At first, Gnedich thought he was being cheated; but when his companion had proved that he now knew Greek, translating several passages taken from Homer at random, he did not know how to express his wonder and admiration in sufficiently strong terms. Afterwards, he induced Krilof to commence a translation of the " Odyssey," but it never went very far. Krilof soon began to neglect his classical studies, and the large collection of Greek works he had bought was shoved under his bed. Sometimes he would stretch out an arm in search of an Æsop, but all the others were forgotten ; and, at last, his housekeeper, seeing no use in such musty volumes, used them up, one after another, to heat the stove. A somewhat similar fate once befell a fable of his own. He had read it aloud at a party, and forgotten to take away the manuscript with him. The next day he sent for it, but learned that the servants, having found a very shabby roll of paper, had used it to wrap up candles in.

As he grew older and more corpulent, his natural laziness increased, and it became difficult to induce him to exert himself. He used to lie in bed late, and, when he got up, he would invest himself in a dressing-gown and a pair of slippers, and often sit in his rooms till evening, dressed in little more than that simple garb. When he was on duty in the Library, and therefore confined within its walls for twenty-four hours, he never grumbled at his lot, as Gnedich used to do, but would lie on a sofa and read novels all day. He read all sorts of trash, merely to kill time, and sometimes thought so little about what he was reading that, when he had got to the end of a story, he would begin it over again without recognising it. The only occurrence which could rouse him to active exertion was that of a fire. The moment he heard of one, he would jump out of bed, and set off for the scene of the disaster, willing to remain intently gazing at it as long as it lasted. He seldom grew so excited in conversation about any other subject as he was when he described the various great fires which he had seen, especially that which took place on the north side of the Neva, when the " camels "

for the ships were destroyed. Conflagrations are numerous
and extensive in Russia, and in winter, when everything is
white with snow, the effects produced by a large mass of
flame at night are very fine, and the more lasting inasmuch
as it is difficult to obtain water in any other shape than that
of rock ice.

Towards the end of Krilof's stay in the Library, he was
recommended by the doctors to take more exercise; so, in
fine weather, he used to go for long walks, and when it
rained he paced the galleries round the upper floor of the
Gostinnoi-Dvor. At first, the shopkeepers used, according
to their wont, to pester him with invitations to purchase;
and, one day, the occupants of a certain stall made a rush at
him, and led him in triumph to their counter. Feigning
acquiescence, he turned over all they showed him; but
always demanded still more costly goods, until he had
made them fairly turn all their stock upside down. Then,
with many thanks for the interesting exhibition they had
offered him, he made his escape. A little farther on, the
same scene was repeated. Then the shopkeepers grew
wiser: those who had been victimized indulged in that little
laugh at their own expense, for which a Russian's sense of
humour makes him almost always ready; and the rest still
more fully appreciated the joke.

Some of Krilof's biographers have spoken as if his personal appearance had been well known to all his fellow-
citizens; but this is evidently a mere figure of speech. One
of them tells a story of how the fabulist was lunching off

oysters one day—he was very fond of them, and it is said that he could dispose of eight dozen, "washed down with English porter"—when he discovered that he had left his purse behind. So he had to ask the proprietor of the establishment, whom he did not know, to give him credit. "Certainly, Ivan Andreëvich," answered the landlord. "What, you know me, then?" asked Krilof. "Of course," was the flattering reply; "every one in the city knows you, Ivan Andreëvich."

So far, so well; but another narrator adds that, as Krilof was on his way home, he stopped to buy some paper at a shop in the Gostinnoi-Dvor, just opposite his own rooms. When the parcel was handed to him, he said to the shop-keeper, "I am Krilof; I live up there. Please send up for the money." But the tradesman, with the unseemly materialism of his class, merely remarked, "How can one know all the people in the world? There's lots of them hereabouts;" and refused to part with the paper until it was paid for.

But, in spite of this tradesman-like ignorance, it is certain that Krilof was well known by sight as well as by reputation; and people used to point him out to each other, and especially to their children, as he walked along the streets. His fables were eagerly sought after by the editors of journals and magazines, and the collected editions of them which he published from time to time met with a large and steadily increasing sale. Between the years 1830 and 1840, the publisher Smirdine printed 40,000 copies of them in various forms, which found their way into all parts of the empire, and made Krilof by far the most popular author of the day. There was scarcely a child belonging to the educated classes who was not familiar with his stories; and they were written in so simple a style, and in such idiomatic language, that they were, for the most part, perfectly intelligible even to the totally uneducated peasant. His sketches of village life, for instance, and his shrewd little illustrations of popular thought and feeling would be as thoroughly appreciated by the rude inhabitants of a hamlet in the interior, supposing that they had an opportunity of hearing them read or recited, as by the literary men whom Krilof used to meet at Jukovsky's pleasant Saturday-evening gatherings, or by his learned colleagues of the Academy of Sciences or the "Society of the Lovers of Russian Literature."

Nor was it merely in his own country that Krilof's name was known. Various translators had given specimens of his writings to their respective countrymen; and, in the year 1824, a sumptuous edition of his fables was edited in Paris by Count Gregory Orlof. A number of distinguished French and Italian poets co-operated in this work, rendering into their best verse the literal prose translations which were laid before them. Many a version which pretends to be "from the Russian" has been really produced after a similar fashion, and the result has generally been as disappointing as that of Count Orlof's enterprise, "whose book," says M. Charles Parfait, "was one in which Russia could not recognise a single characteristic of her national poet." Still it served to

gain Krilof a reputation in France of which many of his contemporaries would have been very proud. He does not seem
to have cared much about it himself; and on one occasion,
when the proofs of a memoir of his life, which was about to
be inserted in a French biographical dictionary, were sent to
him for correction, he at first refused to trouble himself about
them at all, saying, " Let them write what they like," and ultimately consented only to make a few slight alterations in
them. For he was singularly free from that eager thirst after
fame which so many really distinguished writers have felt. He
always spoke most modestly about what he had done. "I am
like a sailor," he said, on one occasion, "who has not met with
any disasters, simply because he has never ventured far from
shore." His early works he called the follies of his youth;
and even of his fables, after they had gained the general
applause of the public, he was wont to say very little. Many
of them alluded to persons and to events about which many
people must have been curious to know ; but he scarcely
ever told even his most intimate friends what were the
particular objects of his satire ; and, in most cases, the
secret went with him into the grave. Of his manuscripts
he was utterly careless. Before a fable was printed, he took
the greatest pains with it, going, perhaps, as many as ten
times over it, and never ceasing to revise it as long as there
was a word in it he could improve or correct. But, after the
printers had finished with his copy, he took no more interest
in it. Of the collection of his manuscripts now in the Public
Library at St. Petersburg, a great part consists of a number

of rough drafts found by his friend Lobanof among the litter of a garret.

In February, 1838, Krilof's seventieth birthday was celebrated by his friends in a manner which could not fail to touch him deeply. A grand banquet was organized in the Nobles' Hall, at which three hundred of the most distinguished members of the cultivated society of St. Petersburg assisted. In front of his seat was placed his bust, crowned with flowers, and, at the end of the feast, flowers were showered down upon him by the ladies who occupied the galleries, and who were eager to do honour to their own and their children's friend. A laurel crown had been presented to him, and, as he was going away, a number of the students of the University crowded round him, asking for a leaf as a relic.

From that time forward, he may almost be said to have written no more. About a couple of years after the festival, he resigned his office, and moved from the Public Library to the other side of the river. There he lived for some time in the Vassily Ostrof, leading a very retired life, and gradually dropping more and more out of society. It was while he was there that a fire broke out, one night, next door. Every one else was naturally much alarmed; but Krilof took everything so quietly, that he would not even dress and go out until he had finished his tea and a cigar, nor would he give any orders about saving his books and memoranda.

After some time, he again changed his abode, and went to the extremity of the city, where he fitted up some rooms, from the windows of which a splendid view might be enjoyed.

There he proposed to lead a still more retired life than before. It would, perhaps, have been more lonely than he would have liked; for he had outlived most of the friends of his younger days, and he does not seem to have had a single relation with whom he was acquainted. At one period of his life, when he was young and poor, and, comparatively speaking, unknown, he had formed a strong attachment for a young girl, whom he hoped to be allowed to marry. But her parents objected to his poverty, and his hopes remained unfulfilled. Among his poems are to be found a number of lyrics addressed to Annette. They form the only trace that is left of the fruitless passion of his youth. In his old age he adopted the children of his servant's daughter, Saveleva; but it is very likely that, in his declining years, he missed those little attentions by which a loved hand can do so much to make smooth the end of the journey of life.

His last illness was one of but short duration. He retained the full use of his faculties to the end; and his last words were, "Lord, forgive me my trespasses!" With them ended a life which was very dear to his countrymen. He died on November $\frac{9}{21}$, 1844, at the age of 76.

His funeral was celebrated at the public expense, and was attended by such crowds that the great church of St. Isaac could not hold those who wished to assist at the service of the dead. The whole of the Nevsky Prospect was thronged by masses of sympathizing lookers-on, thousands of whom followed the coffin, which, surrounded by the students of the University, passed slowly up the long street, and under the windows of the rooms in which Krilof had spent so many peaceful years, till it reached the cemetery attached to the Convent of St. Alexander Nevsky. There the remains of Krilof were deposited, by the side of the tomb of his friend Gnedich, and within sight of that of Karamzine. Beside him in the coffin his friends had placed the laurel crown which had been conferred upon him at the time of his jubilee banquet, and, in accordance with an urgent request which he expressed before his death, a bouquet which had many years previously been presented to him by the Empress Alexandra Fedorovna. Soon afterwards a public subscription was opened for the purpose of erecting a monument to his memory, and the children of Russia, of all ages and classes, united in contributing to it. With its proceeds an excellent statue of the poet was set up in the Summer Garden, within sight of the windows of the palace which now occupies the place of the house in which his printing-press used to work. There he sits in bronze, just as he used to sit in the flesh, clad in his well-loved dressing-gown, an open book in his hand. The pedestal of the monument is adorned with bronze figures representing the various animals about which he wrote ; and a couple of bas-reliefs illustrate two of his most popular fables—"Demian's Fish Soup" and "Fortune and the Beggar." Around the monument, which stands in a circular open space, a number of children are always at play, dressed in the picturesque garb which juvenile Russia affects, and on them the poet seems to smile benignly as he looks down from his easy chair above. It is a thoroughly national monument—a somewhat rare object in Russia, where previous statues have for the most part greatly puzzled the natives, who call them *bolvani*—idols. That of Lomonossof, for instance, which stands at Archangel bareheaded and classically undressed, is a subject of great wonder to the peasants, who find it of a chilly and depressing appearance, as seen among the snows of an Arctic winter. But Krilof's statue is of an altogether different kind, having the merits of being characteristic and intelligible. It is a worthy memorial to a man who had, to a singular degree, gained the affection of his contemporaries, and who will probably retain that of their descendants. For many a score of years to come his memory is likely to be kept green in the minds of the children and the children's children of those little people who now play around his statue, in what is one of the most picturesque spots of St. Petersburg, when the sun is bright and the sky is blue overhead, and the trees of the Summer Garden are clothed in foliage that offers a pleasant shelter from the heat. At such a time it is very pleasant for any one who has read Krilof's fables, and who is not unduly depressed by the thought that the tide of aristocratic life has ebbed from the summer-smitten city, to sit in the grateful shade, and, as he lazily watches the gleam of palace walls through the openings in the hanging curtain of green leaves, to call up before his mental vision the varied scenes which the poet has depicted, and the quaint animal life with which he has peopled them. If it be a Russian who is thus indulging in day-dreams, the chances are that they will be crossed by some shadow of regret for old days gone by, and perhaps haunted by what seem to be echoes of a voice that is still.

KRILOF'S STATUE IN THE SUMMER GARDEN.

THE TWO PEASANTS.

"GOOD day, gossip Thaddeus!"

"Good day, gossip Egor!"

"Well, friend, how are you getting on?"

"Oh, gossip, I see you don't know about my misfortune. God has afflicted me: I have burnt myself out of house and home, and have been obliged to go about begging ever since."

"How ever did you manage that? That was a poor joke, my friend."

"Just so. On Christmas Day we had a feast. I went out to give the horses their food, candle in hand. I must confess there was a buzzing in my head. Well, I don't know how it was, but I must have let a spark fall. I just managed to save myself; but my homestead was burnt, and all I had in it. Now for your story."

"Ah, Thaddeus, a sad piece of work! With me, also, it seems, God has been angry. You see, I have no feet left. I think it's a perfect miracle that I escaped with my life. I went to the cellar for beer. It was Christmas Day in my case too, and I, too, must confess that I had swallowed a little too much brandy along with my friends. Well, that I mightn't set the house on fire in my drunkenness, I blew the candle right out. But the devil gave me such a fall downstairs in the dark, that he made me a mere wreck of a man; and here I've been a cripple ever since."

"Blame yourselves, friends," said their kinsman Stefan. "To tell the truth, I don't think it a miracle that one of you has burnt his house down, and the other is on crutches. Things go ill with a drunken man, when he has a candle in his hand; but he is even worse off when he is in the dark."

THE EDUCATION OF THE LION.

TO the Lion, the king of the forests, Heaven gave a son. You know how different from ours is the nature of beasts. Among us, a child a year old, if it belong to a royal family, is small and weak and stupid. But, by the time it has lived a twelvemonth, a lion-cub has long ago left off its baby-linen. So, at the end of a year, the Lion began seriously to consider that he must not allow his son to remain ignorant, not wishing that the royal dignity should be degraded in him, or that, when the son's turn should come to govern the kingdom, the nation should reproach the father on his account. But whom should he entreat, or compel, or induce by rewards to instruct the Czarevich how to become a Czar?

Should he hand him over to the Fox? The Fox is clever, but it is terribly addicted to telling lies; and a liar is perpetually getting into trouble. "No," thought the Lion ; "the science of falsehood is not one which princes ought to study." Should he trust him to the Mole? Every one who speaks of that animal says that it is an extreme admirer of regularity in everything, and that it never takes a step without examining the ground before it, and that it cleans and shells with its own paws every grain of corn that comes to its table. In fact, the Mole has the reputation of being very great in small affairs. Unfortunately, however, though the Mole's eyes are keen for whatever is just under its nose, it cannot see anything at a distance. The Mole's love of order is an excellent thing for animals of its own kind; but the Lion's kingdom is considerably more extensive than a mole-run. Should he choose the Panther? The Panther is brave and strong, and, besides that, it is a great master of military tactics. But the Panther knows nothing about politics, and is absolutely ignorant of everything else that concerns civil affairs. Pretty lessons indeed it would give in ruling! A king must be a judge and a minister, as well as a warrior; but the Panther is good for nothing but fighting, so it, too, is unfit to educate royal children. To be brief, not a single beast, not even the Elephant himself, who was as much respected in the forest as Plato used to be in Greece, seemed wise enough or sufficiently well informed to satisfy the Lion.

By good fortune, or the opposite—we shall find out which before long,—another king, the king of birds, the Eagle, an old acquaintance and friend of the Lion, heard of that monarch's difficulty, and, wishing to do his friend a great kindness, offered to educate the young Lion himself. The Lion felt as if a weight were taken off his shoulders ; and no wonder. What could be better, as it seemed, than to find a king as a prince's tutor? So the Lion-cub was got ready, and sent off to the Eagle's court, there to learn how to govern.

Two or three years go by; in the meantime, ask whom you will, you hear nothing but unanimous praise of the young Lion, and all the birds scatter through the forests wonderful stories about his merits. At last the appointed time comes, and the Lion sends for his son. The prince arrives, and the king gathers all his people together, summoning great and small alike. He embraces his son before them all, kisses him, and addresses him in these words: " My beloved son, you are my only heir. I am now looking forward to the grave ; but you are only just entering upon life, so I intend to make over my sceptre to you. Only tell me first, in the presence of this assembly, what you have been taught, how much you know, and in what manner you propose to make your people happy."

" Papa," answered the prince, " I know what no one else here knows. I can tell where each bird, from the Eagle to the Quail, can most readily find water, on what each of them lives, and how many eggs it lays ; and I can count up all the wants of every bird, without missing one. Here is the certificate my tutor gave me. It was not for nothing that the birds used to say that I could pick the stars out of the sky.

And when you have made up your mind to transfer your power to me, I will immediately begin to teach the beasts how to make nests."

On this the king and all his beasts howled aloud. The members of the council hung their heads, and the old Lion perceived, too late, that the young Lion had not learned what was wanted—that he was acquainted with birds only, not knowing the nature of beasts, although he was destined by birth to rule over beasts, and that he was utterly ignorant of the knowledge which is most requisite in kings—the knowledge of what are the wants of their own people, and what are the interests of their own country.

[This fable refers to the education of the Emperor Alexander I. Catherine entrusted it to the Genevese La Harpe—a man of excellent intentions, but one who knew very little about Russia, and who set up his own little republic before the eyes of the future despot as the type of the most perfect commonwealth in the world. He filled the boy's head with ideas which would certainly appear to Krilof to be beyond a boy's comprehension; and when his pupil came to the throne, he wrote him a pressing letter from Geneva, urging him to give Russia a constitution, without waiting to make any preparations for its reception.

One of Florian's fables bears the title of "The Lion's Education;" and as it was translated by Dmitrief, it is very probable that Krilof may have read it. But there is very little resemblance between the two fables.]

THE BROOK.

A SHEPHERD by the side of a Brook complainingly
sang, in his grief, of his sad and irreparable loss. His
pet lamb had lately been drowned in the neighbouring river.
Having heard the Shepherd, the Brook thus began to murmur
indignantly:

"Insatiable river! how would it be if thy depths, like
mine, were clearly visible to all eyes, and every one could
see, in thy most secret recesses, all the victims which thou
hast so greedily swallowed up? I think that thou wouldst
dive into the earth for shame, and hide thyself in its dark
abysses. Methinks that, if Fate gave me such copious waters,

I should become an ornament to Nature, and would never hurt even so much as a chicken.   How cautiously should my waves roll past every bush, every cottage !   My shores would only bless me, and I should bring fresh life to the adjacent valleys and meadows, without robbing them of so much as even a single leaflet.   Then, in a word, I should perform my journey in a kindly spirit, nowhere causing misfortune or sorrow, and my waters should flow right down to the sea as pure as silver."

So spake the Brook, and so it really meant.   But what happened ?   A week had not gone by before a heavy rain-cloud burst upon a neighbouring hill.   In its affluence of waters the Brook suddenly rivalled the river.   But, alas ! what has become of the Brook's tranquillity ?   The Brook overflows its banks with turbid waters.   It seethes ; it roars ; it flings about masses of soiled foam.   It overthrows ancestral oaks : their crashing may be heard afar.   And, at last, that very shepherd, on whose account it lately upbraided the river with such a flow of eloquence, perished in it with all his flock, and of his cottage not even a trace was left behind.

How many brooks are there which flow along so smoothly, so peacefully, and murmur so sweetly to the heart, only because they have but very little water in them !

THE MILLER.

THE water began to dribble away through a Miller's dam. At first there would have been no great harm done, if he had taken the matter in hand. But why should he? Our Miller does not think of troubling himself. The leak becomes worse every day, and the water pours out as if from a tap.

"Hallo, Miller! don't stand gaping there! It's time you should set your wits to work."

But the Miller says,

"Harm's a long way off. I don't require an ocean of water, and my mill is rich enough in it for all my time."

He sleeps; but meantime the water goes on running in torrents. And see! harm is here now in full force. The millstone stands still; the mill will not work. Our Miller bestirs himself, groans, troubles himself, and thinks how he can keep the waters back. While he is here on the dam, examining the leak, he observes his fowls coming to drink at the river.

"You stupid, good-for-nothing birds!" he cries. "I don't know where I'm to get water, even when you are out of the question; and here you come and drink the little that remains."

So he begins pelting them with faggots. What good did he do himself by this? Without a fowl left, or a drop of water, he went back home.

I have sometimes remarked that there are many proprietors of this kind — and this little fable was composed as a present for them—who do not grudge thousands spent on follies, but who think that they maintain domestic economy by collecting their candle-ends, and are ready to quarrel with their servants about them. With such economy, is it strange that houses rapidly fall utterly to pieces?

[It is said that Krilof's own ideas of economy were, for the most part, of the very kind he satirizes here. "Returning from a party with me one evening," says his friend Gniedich, "Krilof wouldn't pay what I did for a good carriage, saying it was wasting money. So he walked half of the way home ; but then he became tired, and eventually he was obliged to get into a wretched vehicle, and pay almost as much, for half the distance, as he had been asked at first.   And this was what he called economy."]

THE GRANDEE.

ONCE, in the days of old, a certain Grandee passed from his richly dight bed into the realm which Pluto sways. To speak more simply, he died. And so, as was anciently the custom, he appeared before the justice-seat of Hades. Straightway he was asked, "Where were you born? What have you been?"

"I was born in Persia, and my rank was that of a Satrap. But, as my health was feeble during my lifetime, I never exercised any personal control in my province, but left everything to be done by my secretary."

"But you—what did you do?"

"I ate, drank, and slept; and I signed everything he set before me."

"In with him, then, at once into Paradise!"

"How now! Where is the justice of this?" thereupon exclaimed Mercury, forgetting all politeness.

"Ah, brother," answered Eacus, "you know nothing about it. But don't you see this? The dead man was a fool. What would have happened if he, who had such power in his hands, had unfortunately interfered in business? Why, he would have ruined the whole province. The tears which would have flowed then would have been beyond all calculation. Therefore it is that he has gone into Paradise, because he did not interfere with business."

I was in court yesterday, and I saw a judge there. There can be no doubt that he will go into Paradise.

[When this fable was submitted to the censors, they sent it on to the Minister of Public Instruction, who kept it by him for a whole year, instead of giving any decision about it. Meanwhile, copies of it were circulated in MS., and it became well known in society; but still the minister withheld permission to print it. At last, at one of the court-masquerades, Krilof found an opportunity of reading it to the Emperor Nicholas, who was so delighted with it that he took him in his arms, kissed him, and said, " Write away, old man, write away." On the strength of this, Krilof applied anew to the authorities, and obtained leave to print the fable. With its appearance, his literary career may be said to have come to a close.]

THE WOLF IN THE KENNEL.

A WOLF, one night, thinking to climb into a sheepfold, fell into a kennel. Immediately the whole kennel was up in arms. The dogs, scenting the grisly disturber so near at hand, began to bark in their quarters, and to tear out to the fight.

"Hallo, lads, a thief!" cried the keepers; and immediately the gates were shut. In a moment the kennel became a hell. Men come running, one armed with a club, another with a gun. "Lights!" they cry; "bring lights!" The lights being brought, our Wolf is seen sitting squeezed up in the furthest corner, gnashing its teeth, its hide bristling, and its eyes looking as if it would fain eat up the whole party. Seeing, however, that it is not now in the presence of the flock, and that it is now called upon to pay the penalty for the sheep it has killed, my trickster resorts to negotiation, beginning thus :

"Friends, what is all this fuss about? I am your ancient gossip and comrade; and I have come here to contract an alliance with you—not with the slightest intention of quarrelling. Let us forget the past, and declare in favour of mutual harmony. Not only will I for the future avoid touching the flocks belonging to this spot, but I will gladly fight in their behalf against others; and I swear on the word of a Wolf that I——"

"Listen, neighbour," here interrupted the huntsman. "You are grey-coated; but I, friend, am grey-headed, and I have long known what your wolfish natures are like, and therefore it is my custom never to make peace with wolves until I have torn their skin from off their backs."

With that he let go the pack of hounds on the Wolf.

[This fable, which was printed in October, 1812, represents Napoleon in Russia. The words put into the mouth of the Wolf are almost exactly those of which he himself made use. It is said that, after the battle of Krasnoe, Kutuzof read this fable aloud to the officers who stood round him, and that, when he came to the words, "You are grey-coated; but I, friend, am grey-headed," in which an allusion is made to Napoleon's grey overcoat and his own white hair, he took off his white forage-cap, and shook his bent head. Buistrof says that he once read to Krilof a statement to the effect that, "after Borodino, Kutuzof's young soldiers abused him for not instantly attacking Napoleon ; but Krilof, understanding his intentions, sent him this fable, which he read to his younger officers, and so appeased them." On hearing this, however, Krilof frowned, and said, "That's all nonsense. Is it likely that I, a private individual, neither a diplomatist nor a soldier, should have known beforehand what Kutuzof was going to do? It's absurd! Say, in some paper or other, my friend, that it is not true."]

THE THREE MOUJIKS.

THREE Moujiks * stopped at a village to pass the night.
They had done their business at Petersburg as drivers;
had sometimes worked, and sometimes amused themselves;
and were now going back to their native place. As a Moujik
does not like to go to bed empty, our visitors asked for
supper. But villagers have no variety of dishes. They set
on the table before the hungry travellers a basin of cabbage
soup, some bread, and the remains of a bowl of porridge.
It wasn't like Petersburg fare, but there was no use in talk-

---

* Peasants.

ing about that ; at all events, it was better than going to bed hungry. So the Moujiks crossed themselves, and sat down to table. Then the one who was the sharpest of them, seeing that there was altogether but little for three, perceived how the business might be mended. When force can't win the day, a little cunning must be tried.

"Comrades," he cries, "you know Thomas ; well, he 's likely to have his hair cropped * during this levy."

"What levy ? "

" Why, there 's news of a war with China.   Our father † has ordered the Chinese to pay a tribute of tea."

On that the two others took to weighing the matter, and deliberating upon it (unfortunately they could read, and had studied newspapers and reports), as to how the war would be carried on, and who should have the command. Our friends began a regular discussion, surmised, explained, wrangled. That was just what our trickster wanted.   While they were giving their advice, and settling affairs, and arranging the forces, he didn't say a word, but ate up the whole of the soup and the porridge.

---

*To be taken as a soldier.   † The Emperor.

THE DIVISION.

CERTAIN honest merchants, who had their dwelling and their counting-house in common, made a heap of money. Having wound up their business, they wish to divide their gains. But how can a division take place without squabbling? They have begun to quarrel about the money and the stock, when suddenly there is a cry that the house is on fire.

"Quick, quick, save the goods and the house!" shouts one of them. "Come along; we will settle our accounts afterwards!"

2—2

"Give me another thousand first!" screams a second, "or I will not stir from the spot."

"You have given me two thousand too little!" exclaims a third; "but here are my accounts, all perfectly straight."

"No, no; we protest against such an idea. How, for what, and why, do you claim that?"

Forgetting that the house was on fire, these strange fellows went on squabbling where they were, till they were suffocated by the smoke, and they and their goods were all burnt up together.

[This fable is said to refer to the squabbles which took place among the Russian generals at the time of the French invasion. Count Rostopchin, for instance, withdrew from the Moscow Volunteer Committee simply because it was made dependent on the Volunteer Committee of St. Petersburg. In many cases what was much worse than squabbling took place, some of the officials being charged with having, even at that critical period, "stolen all that could be stolen, the very clothes, the very food of the recruits, of the volunteers, of the prisoners."]

THE CROW AND THE HEN.

WHEN the Prince of Smolensk,* using skill as a wea-
pon against insolence, laid a snare for the modern
Vandals, and left them Moscow for their ruin, then all its
inhabitants, old and young, assembled together without loss
of time, and departed from the city, like a swarm of bees
leaving their hive. On all the disquiet which then took
place a Crow looked down tranquilly from a housetop,
whetting its beak the while.

"What! are not you ready to start, gossip?" cried a Hen
to it from a passing cart. "Why, they say the enemy is at
our very gates."

* Kutusof. He received the title of Smolensky after the battle of Krasnoe.

"What is that to me ?" replied the bird of omen. "I shall remain here quietly. You and your sisters can do as you please. But people don't boil crows, or roast them either; so I shall have no difficulty in living on good terms with the new-comers. It may even happen, perhaps, that I may get some cheese from them, or a stray bone, or something or other. Farewell, my fowl ! a happy journey to you."

The Crow really did stay; but, instead of its gaining anything by doing so, when the time came in which the Prince of Smolensk began to starve his guests, it was itself seized by them, and turned into soup.

[This fable was printed in the magazine called " The Son of the Fatherland," in November, 1812. Towards the end of September in that year, news began to reach St. Petersburg of the miserable state of Napoleon's army. " Eye-witnesses assert," said the preceding number of the magazine, "that the French go out to shoot crows every day, and cannot sufficiently praise their *soupe aux corbeaux."* In the same number appeared a caricature, styled "French crow-soup," representing four grenadiers, wounded, ragged, and emaciated, one of whom is plucking a crow, while the others are getting ready a carving-knife and a saucepan. When Murat's travelling kitchen fell into the hands of the Russians, the saucepans were full of horse and cat flesh. Later on in the retreat, a time came when some of the starving soldiers actually preyed on the dead bodies of their comrades.]

THE PEBBLE AND THE DIAMOND.

A DIAMOND, which some one had lost, lay for some time on the high road. At last it happened that a merchant picked it up. By him it was offered to the king, who bought it, had it set in gold, and made it one of the ornaments of the royal crown. Having heard of this, a Pebble began to make a fuss. The brilliant fate of the Diamond fascinated it; and, one day, seeing a Moujik passing, it besought him thus:

"Do me a kindness, fellow-countryman, and take me with you to the capital. Why should I go on suffering here in rain and mud, while our Diamond is, men say, in honour there? I don't understand why it has been treated with such respect. Side by side with me here it lay so many years; it is just such a stone as I am—my close companion. Do take me! How can one tell? If I am seen there, I too, perhaps, may be found worthy of being turned to account."

The Moujik took the stone into his lumbering cart, and conveyed it to the city. Our stone tumbled into the cart, thinking that it would soon be sitting by the side of the Diamond. But a quite different fate befell it. It really was turned to account, but only to mend a hole in the road.

THE MISER.

A CERTAIN Goblin used to keep watch over a rich treasure buried underground. Suddenly, he was ordered by the ruler of the demons to fly away for many years to the other side of the world. His service was of such a nature, that he was obliged to do as he was bid, whether he liked it or not. Our Goblin fell into a terrible perplexity, wondering how he should preserve his treasure in his absence—who there was to take charge of it. To build a treasure-house, and hire a guardian—that would cost much money. To leave it to itself—that way it might be lost. Impossible to answer for it for a day. Some one might dig it up, and steal it : people are quick at scenting out money.

He worried himself; he pondered over it; and at last an idea came into his head. The master of the house to which he was attached was a terrible Miser. The Goblin, having dug up the treasure, appeared to the Miser, and said,

"Dear master, they have ordered me to go away from your house to a distant land. But I have always been well disposed towards you, so don't refuse to accept this treasure of mine, as a parting token of affection. Eat, drink, and be merry, and spend it without fear; only, when you die, I am to be your sole heir. That is my single stipulation. As for the rest, may destiny grant you health and long life."

He spoke, and was off.

Ten—twenty years went by. Having completed his service, the Goblin flies home to his native land. What does he see? O rapturous sight! The Miser, dead from starvation, lies stretched on the strong box, its key in his hand; and the ducats are all there intact. So the Goblin gets his treasure back again, and rejoices greatly to think that it has had a guardian who did not cost him a single farthing.

[Krilof's remark at the end of this fable is—

"When a miser has money, and yet grudges to pay for food and drink, is he not treasuring up his ducats for a goblin?"

M. Parfait, the author of an excellent French translation of the fables, observes that the same idea has been expressed by a popular French poet, Pierre Dupont, who is not very likely to have read Krilof:

> "Tirez profit de cette fable,
> Vous tous qui rognez sur un liard ;
> Vous thésaurisez pour le diable."

The goblin of the fable is the *domovoi*, or domestic spirit, in whom the Russian peasant has great faith. It is, probably, a near relation of the lubber-fiend which, in Milton's country house,

> "Basks at the fire its hairy strength,"

and of the well-known Scotch bogle, which, when its weary landlord was *flitting* in order to get rid of it, exclaimed, from the centre of the furniture-laden cart, " And I 'm flittin', too."]

THE PIKE AND THE CAT.

A CONCEITED Pike took it into its head to exercise the functions of a cat. I do not know whether the Evil One had plagued it with envy, or whether, perhaps, it had grown tired of fishy fare; but, at all events, it thought fit to ask the Cat to take it out to the chase, with the intention of catching a few mice in the warehouse. "But, my dear friend," Vaska says to the Pike, "do you understand that kind of work? Take care, gossip, that you don't incur disgrace. It isn't without reason that they say, 'The work ought to be in the master's power.'"

"Why really, gossip, what a tremendous affair it is!

Mice, indeed ! Why, I have been in the habit of catching perches ! "

"Oh, very well.   Come along ! "

They went ; they lay each in ambush. The Cat thoroughly enjoyed itself ; made a hearty meal ; then went to look after its comrade. Alas ! the Pike, almost destitute of life, lay there gasping, its tail nibbled away by the mice. So the Cat, seeing that its comrade had undertaken a task quite beyond its strength, dragged it back, half dead, to its pond.

[The Pike, in this fable, represents Admiral Tchichakof, who, although a naval officer, was entrusted with the command of the troops intended to prevent Napoleon from crossing the Berezina during the retreat from Moscow. With this view he was stationed at Borisof ; but the French surprised him there, and drove him out of the place, thereby securing the passage of the river. Sir Robert Wilson says the admiral was at dinner when the enemy broke in upon his rear-guard, captured the whole of his correspondence, and inflicted great loss on his troops.

In the Public Library at St. Petersburg is a collection of caricatures relating to the French invasion of Russia, one of which represents Kutuzof holding one end of a long net ; Napoleon, in the form of a hare, is slipping out at the other end, which is held by Tchichakof, who is exclaiming, "*Je le sauve.*"

Tchichakof is said to have been "an Englishman in charac- ter ;" he had learnt navigation in England, and had married an English woman. "To a sailor's bluntness he added the English reserve;" and this made his countrymen dislike him from the first. After the affair of the Berezina, they despised him also.]

THE ASS AND THE NIGHTINGALE.

AN Ass happened to see a Nightingale, one day, and said to it,

"Listen, my dear. They say you have a great mastery over song. I have long wished very much to hear you sing, and to judge as to whether your talent is really so great."

On this the Nightingale began to make manifest its art—whistled in countless ways, sobbed, sustained notes, passed from one song to another; at one time let her voice die away, and echoed the distant murmur of the languishing reed ; at another, poured through the wood a shower of tiny notes. Then all listened to the favourite singer of Aurora. The breezes died away; the feathered choir was hushed; the cattle lay down on the grass. ·Scarcely breathing, the shepherd revelled in it, and only now and then, as he listened to it, smiled on the shepherdess.

At length the singer ended. Then the Ass, bending its head towards the ground, observed,

"It's tolerable. To speak the truth, one can listen to you without being bored. But it's a pity you don't know our Cock. You would sing a great deal better if you were to take a few lessons from him."

Having heard such a judgment, our poor Nightingale took to its wings and flew far away.

[It is said that Krilof wrote this fable after an interview with some great man (Count Razumofsky or Prince A. N. Galitzin, perhaps), who had asked him to read him some of his fables. After hearing them, the noble patron of letters said, "That is very good; but why don't you translate, as Dmitrief does?" "I cannot," modestly answered the poet, who returned home, and straightway wrote down the grandee an ass.

M. Fleury ranks this piece among the imitations; and it is true that the same subject has been admirably treated by Diderot. But the idea may easily have occurred to Krilof without his having read Diderot's excellent fable.]

THE HOP-PLANT.

A HOP-PLANT had made its way to the edge of a garden, and had begun to wind itself around a dry stake
in the fence. Now, in the open field beyond stood an oak-
sapling.

"What use is there in that stunted creature, or, indeed, in any
of its kind?" Thus about the oak the Hop used to whisper
to the stake. "How can it even be compared with you?
You, simply by your erect carriage, look like a perfect lady in
its presence. It is true that it is clothed with foliage; but
how rough it is! what a colour it has! Why ever does the
earth nourish it?"

Meanwhile, a week had scarcely passed, before the owner
broke up that stake for firewood, and transplanted the young
oak into his garden. His care resulted in full success, and
the oak flourished, extending vigorous shoots. Remarking
this, our Hop-plant wound itself about it, and now its voice
is entirely devoted to the oak's glory and honour.

TRISHKA'S CAFTAN.

TRISHKA'S caftan was out at elbows. Why should he ponder long over it? He took to his needle, cut a quarter off each sleeve; so mended the elbows. The caftan was all right again, only his arms were bare for a quarter of their length. That is no great matter; but every one is always laughing at Trishka. So Trishka says,

"As I'm no fool, I'll set this affair straight also. I'll make the sleeves longer than they were before. Oh! Trishka is no common-place fellow."

So he cut off the skirts of his caftan, and used them to lengthen his sleeves. Then Trishka was happy, though he had a caftan which was as short as a waistcoat.   In a similar way have I sometimes seen other embarrassed people set their affairs straight.   Take a look at them as they dash away. They have all got on Trishka's caftan.

[An allusion to the ruinous shifts to which the Russian proprietors used to have recourse when their affairs became at all embarrassed.   They are beginning to be less improvident now; but, at the time when Krilof wrote the fable, they used to be notorious for their readiness to adopt any means which would afford them a temporary relief.   It may easily be imagined how the unfortunate peasants must have suffered whenever their masters were seized by one of these reckless fits.]

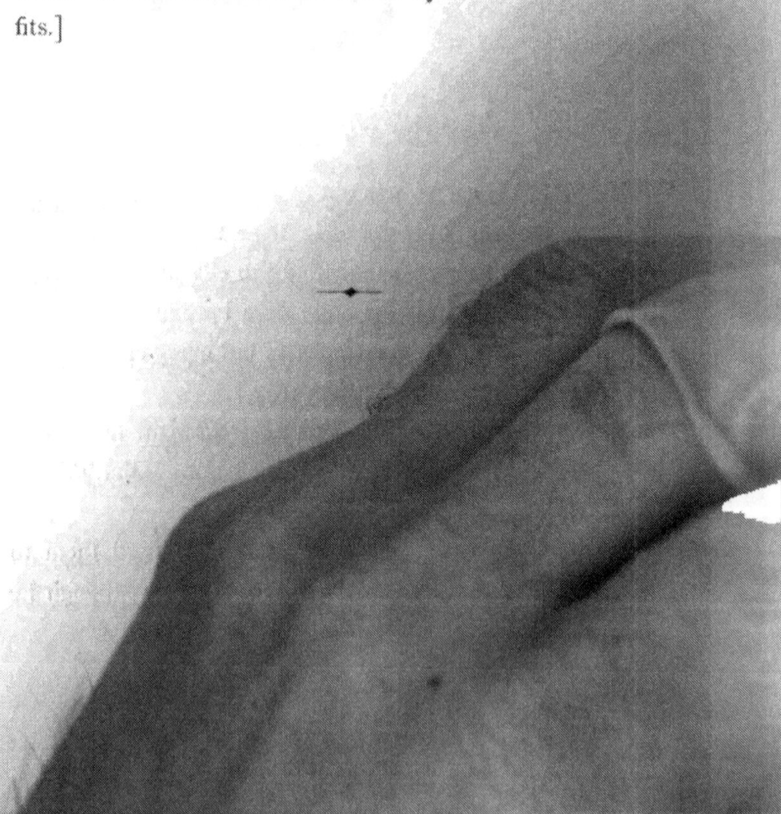

THE ELEPHANT AS GOVERNOR.

A N Elephant was once appointed ruler of a forest. Now, it is well known that the race of elephants is endowed with great intelligence; but every family has its unworthy scion. Our Governor was as stout as the rest of his race are, but as foolish as the rest of his race are not. As to his character, he would not intentionally hurt a fly. Well, the worthy Governor becomes aware of a petition laid before him by the Sheep, stating that their skins are entirely torn off their backs by the Wolves.

"Oh, rogues!" cries the Elephant, "what a crime! Who gave you leave to plunder?"

3—2

But the Wolves say,

"Allow us to explain, O father. Did not you give us leave to take from the Sheep a trifling contribution* for our pelisses in winter? It is only because they are stupid sheep that they cry out. They have only a single fleece taken from each of them, but they grumble about giving even that!"

"Well, well," says the Elephant, "take care what you do. I will not permit any one to commit injustice. As it must be so, take a fleece from each of them. But do not take from them a single hair besides."

He who has rank and power, but wants sense, however good his heart may be, is sure to do harm.

---

* *Obrok*--the tax levied on the peasant by his master.

THE POOR MAN ENRICHED.

"IS IT worth while being rich, if one is never to eat or drink delicately, and to do nothing but heap up money? And to what end? We die, and then leave all behind. We only torment ourselves, and get a bad name. No; if riches had fallen to my share, not only roubles, but even thousands of them wouldn't have been grudged by me, so long as I could live sumptuously and luxuriously; and my feasts should have been talked about far and wide. Besides, I should have done good to others. To rich misers, their life is a kind of torment."

So reasoned a Poor Man with himself, lying on the bare boards in a wretched hovel. Suddenly, gliding to his side through a chink, there appeared—some say a wizard, others say the Evil One (most likely the latter, as the end of the story will show), and began to speak thus:

"You wish to be rich; I have heard you say why. I am glad to help a friend, so here is a purse for you; there is a ducat in it—no more. But, as soon as you have taken one coin out of it, you will find another in it all ready for you. So now, my friend, your growing rich depends entirely upon your own wishes. Take the purse, and freely supply yourself from it until your craving is satisfied. Only bear this in mind,—until you shall have flung the purse into the river, you are forbidden to spend a single ducat."

He spoke, and left the purse with the Poor Man. The Poor Man was almost beside himself for joy. But, as soon as he returned to his senses, he began to handle the purse; and with what result? Scarcely could he believe it was not a dream. He had hardly taken one ducat out, before another was already stirring in the purse. Our needy friend says to himself,

"I will shake out a heap of ducats. Then, to-morrow I shall be rich, and I will begin to live like a Sybarite."

But the next morning he had changed his mind.

"It's true," he says, "I am rich now. But who isn't glad to get hold of a good thing? and why shouldn't I become twice as rich? It surely wouldn't be laziness in me to spend another day over the purse. Here I have money for a mansion, an equipage, a country house. But if I might buy estates too, wouldn't it be stupid in me to lose such an opportunity? Yes, I will keep the wonderful purse. So be it : I will fast one day more. As to that, I shall always have time enough for luxurious living."

But what happens? A day goes by, and then a week, a month, a year. Our Poor Man has long ago lost all count of the ducats. Meanwhile, he eats scantily, and drinks scantily. Scarcely has the day begun to break before he is back at the old work. The day comes to an end; but, according to his calculations, something or other is still sure to be wanting. Sometimes he makes up his mind to throw

away the purse.   But then his heart grows faint within him.
He reaches the bank of the river, and—then turns back
again.

"How can I possibly part with the purse," he says,
"while it yields a stream of gold of its own accord?"

By this time our poor friend has grown grey, and thin,
and as yellow as his own gold.   He no more so much as
thinks about luxury now.   He has become faint and feeble ;
health and rest have utterly deserted him.   But still with
trembling hand he goes on taking ducats out of the purse.
He takes, and takes; and how does it all end?   On the
bench on which he used to sit gloating over his wealth—on
that very bench he dies, in the act of counting the last coins
of his ninth million.

THE QUARTETTE.

THE tricksy Monkey, the Goat, the Ass, and bandy-legged Mishka the Bear, determine to play a quartette. They provide themselves with the necessary pieces of music—with two fiddles, and with an alto and a counter-bass. Then they sit down on a meadow under a lime-tree, prepared to enchant the world by their skill. They work away at their fiddlesticks with a will; and they make a noise, but there is no music in it.

"Stop, brothers, stop!" cries the Monkey, "wait a little! How can we get our music right? It's plain, you mustn't sit as you are. You, Mishka, with your counter-bass, face the alto. I will sit opposite the second fiddle. Then a different sort of music will begin: we shall set the very hills and forests dancing."

So they change places, and recommence ; but the music is just as discordant as before.

" Stop a little," exclaims the Ass; " I have found out the secret. We shall be sure to play in tune if we sit in a row."

They follow its advice, and form in an orderly line. But the quartette is as unmusical as ever. Louder than before there arose among them squabbling and wrangling as to how they ought to be seated. It happened that a Nightingale came flying that way, attracted by their noise. At once they all intreat it to solve their difficulty.

" Be so kind," they say, " as to bear with us a little, in order that our quartette may come off properly. Music we have; instruments we have: tell us only how we ought to place ourselves."

But the Nightingale replies,

" To be a musician, one must have a quicker intelligence and a finer ear' than you possess. You, my friends, may place yourselves just as you like, but you will never become musicians."

[Some writers say this fable alludes to the foundation, in March, 1811, of the " Society of Lovers of Russian Litera-ture," which had four departments, and seemed more like a public office than a literary institution, and the members of which had places allotted to them according to their rank

rather than to their talents.   But Baron Korf says it refers
to the disputes about places which arose among the firs
Presidents of the four departments of the Imperial Council,
at the time of its reconstruction, in the year 1810.]

THE INQUISITIVE MAN.

"GOOD day, dear friend ; where do you come from ?"
"From the Museum, where I have spent three hours. I saw everything they have there, and examined it carefully. So much have I seen to astonish me, that, if you will believe me, I am neither strong enough nor clever enough to give you a full description of it. Upon my word it is a palace of wonders. How rich Nature is in invention ! What birds and beasts haven't I seen there ! What flies, butterflies, cockroaches, little bits of beetles !—some like emeralds, others like coral. And what tiny cochineal insects ! Why, really, some of them are smaller than a pin's head."

"But did you see the elephant ? What did you think it looked like ? I 'll be bound you felt as if you were looking at a mountain."

"Are you quite sure it 's there ?"

"Quite sure."

"Well, brother, you mustn't be too hard upon me ; but, to tell the truth, I didn't remark the elephant."

[Bulgarine states that Krilof wrote this fable in allusion to the remark of some one, perhaps Prince Viazemsky, that each of the three great fabulists, La Fontaine, Khemnitser, and Dmitrief, bore the name of Ivan,—thus omitting all notice of Ivan Krilof. But the story does not seem to rest on any substantial authority, and it is entirely out of keeping with all the other anecdotes about Krilof, who was remarkably modest and unpretentious.]

THE COOK AND THE CAT.

A CERTAIN Cook, rather more educated than his fellows, went from his kitchen one day to a neighbouring tavern —he was of a serious turn of mind, and on that day he celebrated the anniversary of a friend's death—leaving a Cat at home, to guard his viands from the mice. On his return, what does he see? The floor strewed with fragments of a pie, and Vaska the Cat crouching in a corner behind a vinegar-barrel, purring with satisfaction, and busily engaged in disposing of a chicken.

"Ah, glutton! ah, evil-doer!" exclaims the reproachful Cook. "Are you not ashamed of being seen by these walls, let alone living witnesses?   What! be an honourable Cat up to this time—one who might be pointed out as a model of discretion!   And now, ah me! how great a disgrace! Now all the neighbours will say, 'The cat Vaska is a rogue; the cat Vaska is a thief. Vaska must not be admitted into the kitchen, not even into the courtyard, any more than a ravenous wolf into the sheepfold.   He is utterly corrupt; he is a pest, the plague of the neighbourhood.'"

Thus did our orator, letting loose the current of his words, lecture away without stopping.   But what was the result? While he was delivering his discourse, Vaska the Cat ate up the whole of the chicken.

I would advise some cooks to inscribe these words on their walls: "Don't waste time in useless speech, when it is action that is needed."

THE MUSICIANS.

A CERTAIN man invited a neighbour to dinner, not without an ulterior purpose. He was fond of music, and he entrapped his neighbour into his house to listen to his choir. The honest fellows began to sing, each on his own account, and each with all his might. The guest's ears began to split, and his head to turn.

"Have pity on me!" he exclaimed, in amazement. "What can any one like in all this? Why, your choristers bawl like madmen."

"It's quite true," replied the host, with feeling. "They do flay one's ears just a trifle. But, on the other hand, they are all of irreproachable behaviour, and they never touch a drop of intoxicating liquor."

But, I say, in my opinion you had better drink a little, if needs be : only take care to understand your business thoroughly.

THE PEASANT AND THE LABOURER.

AN old Peasant and a Labourer were going home through the forest to the village one evening, in the time of the hay-harvest, when they suddenly found themselves face to face with a bear. Scarcely had the Peasant time to utter a cry when the bear was upon him; it threw him down, rolled him over, made his bones crack again, and began looking about for a soft spot at which to commence its meal. Death draws near to the old man.

"Stefan, my kinsman, my dear friend, do not desert me!" he cries, from under the bear, to the Labourer.

Then Stefan, putting forth all his strength like a new

Hercules, splits the bear's head in two with his axe, and drives his pitchfork into its bowels. The bear howls, and falls dying. Our bear expires.

The danger having vanished, the Peasant gets up, and soundly scolds the Labourer. Our poor Stefan is astounded.

" Pardon me, what have I done ? "

" What have you done, you blockhead ? I 'd like to know what you are so absurdly pleased about ; why, you 've gone and stuck the bear in such a manner that you 've utterly ruined his fur ! "

THE BEAR AMONG THE BEES.

THE beasts elected the Bear, one spring, Inspector of the Beehives. They might, it is true, have chosen a more trustworthy animal, seeing that the Bear is passionately fond of honey. The matter was one to be regretted ; but who can expect wisdom from beasts? Every other solicitor for the post of Hive Inspector they sent away with a refusal, and finally, as if by way of pleasantry, the Bear made his appearance in that capacity. But harm soon came of the appointment for our Bear carried off all the honey into his den. The theft was found out, an alarm was sounded, and legal proceedings were taken in due form. Eventually, the

Bear was dismissed from his office, and the old rogue was sentenced to lie in his den all the winter.

The Court decided, ratified, and countersigned; but, in spite of all this, it did not return the honey. As for Mishka, he didn't pay the slightest attention to the affair. Bidding the world farewell for a season, he betook himself to his warm den. There he sucks his honeyed paw, and waits till fair weather invites him to a fresh cruise.

[At the time when Krilof wrote, extortion and corruption were scandalously rife in Russia. The Government strove hard to put down the extortioners, and the Press did all that it could, in its fettered condition, to aid in so good a cause. But, in spite of all that could be done, the evil went on flourishing. As soon as Alexander I. came to the throne, he issued an edict against exactions of every kind; and in 1809, when the great abuses in the Commissariat Department had been brought to light, he renewed the old ukases of Peter the Great and Catherine II. The first, published in 1714, orders that all persons convicted of extorting money and taking bribes shall undergo severe corporal punishment, shall forfeit all their property, and shall be " treated as rascals, and turned out of the list of honest people." The second, of the date of 1763, ordains that they shall be " not only turned out of the ranks of honest people, but eliminated from the entire human race." But, notwithstanding all these energetic declarations, the forbidden practices remained unchecked; and, to the end of Alexander's reign, each year saw a new edict issued on the subject. In 1816, especially, a vigorous attempt was made to produce a reform, and a rescript was addressed to the Minister of Justice, bidding him see that the law courts should be rendered the means of maintaining right, not of confirming wrong ; and that assistance should be given to the weak and needy in their appeals against oppression. But it too often occurred that, when some great man had been detected in robbing the poor, the only punishment he underwent was a nominal banishment to his estates, where he enjoyed, like the Bear, the fruits of his villany, and waited till the temporary ill wind should have blown over.]

THE HORSE AND THE DOG.

A DOG and a Horse, which served the same peasant, began to discuss each other's merits, one day.

"How grand we are, to be sure!" says Barbos. "I shouldn't be sorry if they were to turn you out of the farm-yard. A noble service, indeed, to plough or to draw a cart! And I've never heard of any other proof of your merit. How can you possibly compare yourself with me? I rest neither by day nor by night. In the daytime I watch the cattle in the meadows; by night I guard the house."

"Quite true," replied the Horse. "What you say.is perfectly correct. Only remember that, if it weren't for my ploughing, you wouldn't have anything at all to guard here."

DEMIAN'S FISH SOUP.

"NEIGHBOUR, light of my eyes ! do eat a little more."
"Dear neighbour, I am full to the throat.'
"No matter ; just a little plateful.   Believe me, the soup
is cooked gloriously."
"But I 've had three platefuls already."
"Well, what does that matter ?   If you like it and it does
you good, why not eat it all up ?   What a soup it is !   How
rich !   It looks as if it had been sprinkled over with amber.
Here is bream ; there is a lump of sterlet.   Take a little more,
dear, kind friend.   Just another spoonful ! Wife, come and
intreat him."

Thus does Demian feast his neighbour Phocas, not giving

him a moment's breathing-time.   Phocas feels the moisture
trickling down his forehead ; still he takes one more plateful,
attacks it with all the strength he has left, and somehow
manages to swallow the whole of it.

"That's the sort of friend I like !" cries Demian. "I can't
bear people who require pressing. But now, dear friend,
take just one little plateful more !"

But, on hearing this, our poor Phocas, much as he liked
fish soup, catching hold of his cap and sash, runs away home
without looking behind him.   Nor from that day to this has
he crossed Demian's threshold.

[There was a meeting one day, at the house of the poet
Derjavine, of the members of the " Society of the Lovers of
Russian Literature." Krilof had promised to attend, and to
read one of his new and, as yet, unpublished fables ; but he
did not appear till very late. When he arrived, some one was
reading an exceedingly long poem, which went on and on
until the audience was utterly worn out.   At last, however,
it came to an end. Then Krilof was asked to read his poem ;
so he put his hand in his pocket, produced a piece of paper,
and read " Demian's Fish Soup." It is easy to imagine how
thoroughly it was appreciated by an audience which had just
been suffering tortures at the hands of a literary Demian—
one of those authors who, when they have once secured a
hearing, never know when it is time to leave off.]

THE WOLVES AND THE SHEEP.

THE Sheep could not live in peace on account of the
Wolves, and the evil increased to such a pitch, that at
last the rulers of the beasts had to take vigorous steps towards
interfering and saving the victims. With that intent a council
was summoned. The majority of its members, it is true,
were Wolves; but then all Wolves are not badly spoken of.
There have been Wolves known, and that often (such
instances are never forgotten), to have walked past a flock
quite peacefully—when completely gorged. So why should
not Wolves have seats in the council? Although it was
necessary to protect the Sheep, yet there was no reason for
utterly suppressing the Wolves.

Well, the meeting took place in the thick wood. They
pondered, considered, harangued, and at last framed a decree.
Here you have it, word for word :—" As soon as a Wolf
shall have disturbed a flock, and shall have begun to worry
a Sheep, then the Sheep shall be allowed, without respect
to persons, to seize it by the scruf of the neck, to carry it
into the nearest thicket or wood, and there to bring it before
the court."

This law is everything that can be desired. Only, I have
remarked, up to the present day, that although the Wolves

are not to be allowed to worry with impunity, yet in all cases, whether the Sheep be plaintiff or defendant, the Wolf is always sure, in spite of all opposition, to carry off the Sheep into the forest.

THE MAN AND HIS SHADOW.

THERE was a certain original who must needs desire to catch his own Shadow. He makes a step or two towards it, but it moves away before him. He quickens his pace; it does the same. At last he takes to running; but the quicker he goes, the quicker runs the Shadow also, utterly refusing to give itself up, just as if it had been a treasure. But see! our eccentric friend suddenly turns round, and walks away from it. And presently he looks behind him; the Shadow runs after him now.

Ladies fair, I have often observed——what do you suppose?—no, no; I assure you I am not going to speak about you——that Fortune treats us in a similar way.　One man tries with all his might to seize the goddess, and only loses his time and his trouble.　Another seems, to all appearance, to be running out of her sight ; but, no : she herself takes a pleasure in pursuing him.

THE WOLF AND ITS CUB.

A WOLF, which had begun to accustom its Cub to support itself by its father's profession, sent it one day to prowl about the skirts of the wood. At the same time it ordered it to give all its attention to seeing whether it would not be possible, even at the cost of sinning a little, for them both to make their breakfast or dinner at the expense of some shepherd or other. The pupil returns home, and says—

"Come along, quick! Our dinner awaits us: nothing could possibly be safer. There are sheep feeding at the foot of yon hill, each one fatter than the other. We have only to choose which to carry off and eat; and the flock is so large that it would be difficult to count it over again——"

"Wait a minute," says the Wolf. "First of all I must know what sort of a man the shepherd of this flock is."

"It is said that he is a good one—painstaking and intelligent. But I went round the flock on all sides, and examined the dogs: they are not at all fat, and seem to be spiritless and indolent."

"This description," says the old Wolf, "does not greatly attract me to the flock. For, decidedly, if the shepherd is good, he will not keep bad dogs about him.   One might very soon get into trouble there.   But come with me : I will take you to a flock where we shall be in less danger of losing our skins.   Over that flock it is true that a great many dogs watch ; but the shepherd is himself a fool.   And where the shepherd is a fool, there the dogs too are of little worth."

THE DANCING FISH.

HAVING waters as well as woods in his dominions,
the Lion called the beasts together to a council, to
consider who should be appointed governor of the Fish.
They gave their votes in the usual manner, and the Fox was
chosen. Well, the Fox sat in the governor's seat, and visibly
waxed fat. He had a Moujik as friend, kinsman, and gossip,
and the two used to lay their heads together. The Fox
conducted business and pronounced legal decisions on the
shore ; and meantime his gossip angled after the Fish, and,
like a trusty comrade, shared what he caught with his friend.

But rogues do not always succeed. The Lion somehow

grew suspicious, from rumours it heard, that the scales had been falsified in its law courts; so, having found a leisure time, it determined to investigate the state of its dominions.

Having gone to the shore, it found that the good gossip had caught some fish, and had kindled a fire by the river-side, intending to feast on them with his comrade. The poor fish were bounding into the air to get away from the heat, each one to the best of its power: each one, seeing its end close at hand, flung itself about, gaping at the Moujik.

"Who are you, and what are you doing?" angrily asked the Lion.

"Great king!" answers the chief rogue—the Fox always has a trick in reserve—"great king! this is my chief secretary here, who is esteemed for his probity by all the nation; and these are carp, all inhabitants of the waters. We have all come here to congratulate you, our good king, on your arrival."

"Well, how is justice dispensed here? Is your district content?"

"Great king! here they do not merely live; they are in Paradise. If only your royal life may be prolonged!" (All this time the fish were leaping about in the pan.)

"But tell me," said the Lion, "why do they fling themselves about topsy-turvy in this manner?"

"O wise Lion," replied the Fox, "they are dancing for joy at seeing you."

Not being able to stand such a manifest fiction as this, the Lion, in order that there should be some music for its subjects to dance to, made the secretary and the governor both sing out under its claws.

[This fable, as originally written by Krilof, ended as follows :

" O wise Lion," replied the Fox, " they are dancing for joy at seeing you." Then the Lion, tapping the Starost kindly on the breast, proceeded on his journey.

But the censor objected that this seemed like a reflection on the Emperor Alexander, who was then—it was in the year 1824—making what was destined to be his last journey through Russia. Krilof at first refused to make any alteration ; but eventually he modified the fable, and added the lines with which it now concludes.

There is a tradition that, during one of his travels in the interior, the Emperor Alexander I. spent a night, in some city or other, in the governor's house. The next morning, just as he was on the point of continuing his journey, he happened to look out of window, and saw a great crowd collected in front of the house. The governor, being asked what was the cause of it, replied that it was a deputation of the inhabitants, who wished to thank the Emperor for the happy lives they led. As the Emperor was in a hurry to get away, he declined to receive the deputation, and drove off.

Afterwards it turned out that the people had come to complain of their governor, who oppressed them terribly.]

THE PIKE.

AN appeal to justice was made against the Pike, on the
ground that it had rendered the pond uninhabitable.
A whole cart-load of proofs were tendered as evidence ; and
the culprit, as was beseeming, was brought into court in a
large tub.   The judges were assembled not far off, having
been set to graze in a neighbouring field.   Their names are
still preserved in the archives.   There were two Donkeys,
a couple of old Horses, and two or three Goats.   The Fox
also was added to their number, as assessor, in order that the
business might be carried on under competent supervision.

Now, popular report said that the Pike used to supply the
table of the Fox with fish.   However this might be, there
was no partiality among the judges ; and it must also be
stated that it was impossible to conceal the Pike's roguery
in the affair in question. So there was no help for it. Sentence
was passed, condemning the Pike to an ignominious punishment.   In order to frighten others, it was to be hung from a
tree.

"Respected judges," thus did the Fox begin to speak,
"hanging is a trifle.   I should have liked to have sentenced
the culprit to such a punishment as has never been seen here
among us.   In order that rogues may in future live in fear,
and run a terrible risk, I would drown it in the river."

"Excellent !" cry the judges, and unanimously accept
the proposition.

So the Pike was flung—into the river.

THE GEESE.

A PEASANT, with a long rod in his hand, was driving some Geese to a town where they were to be sold; and, to tell the truth, he did not treat them over-politely. In hopes of making a good bargain, he was hastening on so as not to lose the market-day (and when gain is concerned, geese and men alike are apt to suffer). I do not blame the peasant; but the Geese talked about him in a different spirit, and, whenever they met any passers-by, abused him to them in such terms as these:

"Is it possible to find any Geese more unfortunate than we are? This Moujik harasses us so terribly, and chases us about just as if we were common Geese. The ignoramus does not know that he ought to pay us reverence, seeing that we are the noble descendants of those geese to whom Rome was once indebted for her salvation, and in whose honour even feast-days were specially appointed there."

"And do you want to have honour paid you on that account?" a passer-by asked them.

" Why, our ancestors——"

" I know that—I have read all about it; but I want to know this—of what use have you been yourselves?"

" Why, our ancestors saved Rome!"

" Quite so; but what have you done?"

" We? Nothing."

" Then what merit is there in you? Let your ancestors rest in peace—they justly received honourable reward; but you, my friends, are only fit to be roasted!"

It would be easy to make this fable still more intelligible; but I am afraid of irritating the Geese.

THE LION AND THE PANTHER.

ONCE on a time, in ancient days, the Lion maintained a very long contest with the Panther about certain disputed forests, valleys, and caves. To go to law about their rights—this was not in accordance with their characters; for, in matters relating to law, the strong are often blind. For such affairs they have their own rule,—"Who conquers is right." But at last, that they might not eternally squabble, with claws ever becoming more blunt, our heroes determined to submit their dispute to law. Their intention was to put an end to their fighting, to settle all hostilities, and then, as is customary, to conclude a peace which should last uninterrupted—until the next quarrel.

"Let us each choose a secretary at once," proposes the Panther to the Lion, "and decide according as the two secretaries shall advise. I, for instance, will choose the Cat. It is not a very good-looking little animal; but, then, its conscience is clear. But do you, for your part, nominate the Ass, for it belongs to a distinguished order in the state; and, to tell the truth, you will have in it a very enviable beast. Trust me as a friend in this. All your court and council together are scarcely worth its hoof. Let us accept whatever arrangements it and my Cat may make."

And the Lion sanctioned the first part of the Panther's scheme without opposition ; only he chose the Fox, instead of the Ass, to represent him in the discussion, saying to himself, after so doing,

"Truly, there is but little good to be gained from him whom an enemy recommends."

THE COMB.

A LOVING mother bought a good strong Comb to keep
her boy's hair in order. The child never let his new
present go out of his hands. Whether playing or learning
his alphabet, he was always lovingly passing his Comb through
the twining curls of his waving golden hair, soft as fine flax.
And what a Comb it was! Not only did it not pull out his
hair, but it never even got caught in it; so smoothly and
easily did it glide through his locks. It was a priceless Comb
in the eyes of the child. But at last it happened, one day,
that the Comb was mislaid. Our boy went playing and

romping about, until he got his hair into a regular tangle.
Scarcely had the nurse touched it, when he began to howl,

" Where is my Comb ? "

At last it was found; but when they tried to pass it through
his locks, it could not be moved either backwards or forwards:
all it did was to pull his hair out by the roots, so as to bring
the tears into his eyes.

" How wicked you are, you bad Comb ! " cries the boy.

But the Comb replies,

" My dear, I am what I always was ; only your hair has
become tangled."

Whereupon our young friend, giving way to rage and vexation, flings his Comb into the river.   And now the Naiads
comb their hair with it.

In my time I have often seen men behave in a like manner towards the truth.   As long as we have a clear conscience,
truth is agreeable to us, we hold it sacred, we listen to it and
obey it ; but as soon as a man has begun to do violence to
his conscience, the truth becomes alien to his ears.   Then
every one resembles the boy who did not like to have his
hair combed after it had got into a tangle.

THE AUTHOR AND THE ROBBER.

IN the gloomy realm of shadows, two sinners appeared before the judges for sentence at the very same time. The one was a Robber, who used to extract tribute on the highway, and who had at last come to the gallows ; the other an Author, covered with glory, who had infused a subtle poison into his works, had promoted atheism, and had preached immorality, being, like the Siren, sweet-voiced, and, like the Siren, dangerous. In Hades judical ceremonies are brief ; there are no useless delays. Sentence was pronounced immediately. Two huge iron cauldrons were suspended in the air by two tremendous iron chains ; in each of these one of the sinners was placed. Under the Robber a great pile of wood was heaped up, and then one of the Furies herself set it on fire, kindling such a terrible flame, that the very stone in the roof of the infernal halls began to crack. The Author's sentence did not seem to be a severe one. Under him, at first, a little fire scarcely glowed ; but, the longer it burned, the larger it became.

Centuries have now gone by, but the fire has not gone out. Beneath the Robber the flame has long ago been extinguished ; beneath the Author it grows hourly worse and worse. Seeing that there is no mitigation of his torments, the writer at last cries out amidst them that there is no justice among the gods; that he had filled the world with his renown; and that, if he had written a little too freely, he had been punished too much for it; and that he did not think he had sinned more than the Robber.   Then before him, in all her ornaments, with snakes hissing amid her hair, and with bloody scourges in her hands, appeared one of the three Infernal Sisters.

"Wretch!" she exclaims, "dost thou upbraid Providence? Dost thou compare thyself with this robber?   His crime is as nothing compared with thine.   Only as long as he lived did his cruelty and lawlessness render him hurtful.   But thou —long ago have thy bones turned to dust, yet the sun never rises without bringing to light fresh evils of which thou art the cause.   The poison of thy writings not only does not weaken, but, spreading abroad, it becomes more malignant as years roll by.   Look there!" and for a moment she enables him to look upon the world; "behold the crimes, the misery, of which thou art the cause.   Look at those children who have brought shame upon their families, who have reduced their parents to despair.   By whom were their heads and hearts corrupted?   By thee.   Who strove to rend asunder the bonds of society, ridiculing as childish follies all ideas of the sanctity of marriage and the right of authority and law, and rendering them responsible for all human misfortunes? Thou art the man!   Didst thou not dignify unbelief with the name of enlightenment?   Didst thou not place vice and passion in the most charming and alluring of lights?   And now look!—a whole country, perverted by thy teaching, is full of murder and robbery, of strife and rebellion, and is being led onwards by thee to ruin. For every drop of that country's tears and blood thou art to blame. And now dost thou dare to hurl thy blasphemies against the gods? How much evil have thy books yet to bring upon the world? Continue, then, to suffer; for here the measure of thy punishment shall be according to thy deserts." Thus spoke the angry Fury, and slammed down the cover on the cauldron.

[There seems to be little doubt that Krilof was thinking of Voltaire when he wrote this somewhat violent diatribe. "We prefer to believe," says the French translator of Krilof, in a note on this passage, "that, in spite of his errors, the apostle of universal toleration, the ardent promoter of so many useful and humane reforms, the zealous defender of so many innocent persons, will find less severity in his real Judge than he finds here in the Minos of the fable."]

THE HIND AND THE DERVISH.

A YOUNG Hind, bereft of her much-loved fawns, and still having her udders full of milk, found two young wolves deserted in a forest, and immediately began to fulfil the sacred duty of a mother towards them, feeding them with her milk. A Dervish, who inhabited the same forest, astonished at this proceeding of hers, cried out—

"Imprudent creature that thou art! On what kind of animal art thou conferring thy milk? on what art thou wasting thy affections? Is it possible that thou canst expect gratitude from such as they are? Or is it that thou dost not know their evil nature? Some day, perhaps, it will be thy blood that they will drink."

"It may be so, indeed," replied the Hind; "but I did not think, nor do I wish to think, of that. It is only as a mother that I care to feel just now; and my milk would have been a burden to me if I had not given suck to these little ones."

Thus genuine charity does good without thinking of recompense. To the really benevolent, their abundance would be burdensome if they could not share it with those who are in want.

CANINE FRIENDSHIP.

UNDER a kitchen window lay Barbos and Polkan, basking in the sunshine.   It would have been more fitting in them to have been guarding the house at the gate in front of the courtyard. But they had eaten till they were satiated, and, besides, polite dogs do not bark at any one in the daytime. So they indulged in a discussion about all sorts of things—about their doggish service, about good and evil, and finally about friendship.

"What," says Polkan, "can be pleasanter than to live heart to heart with a friend?—in everything to offer mutual service; not to sleep or eat without one's friend, and to defend his body with all one's force ; finally, for friends to look into one another's eyes, and each to think that only a fortunate hour in which he could please or amuse his friend, and to place all his own happiness in his friend's good fortune ! Suppose, for instance, you and I were to contract such a friendship. I venture to say, we should not be able to tell how quickly time was flying."

"That is true.   So be it," replies Barbos.   "Long has it been grievous to me, my dear Polkan, that we, who are dogs of the same yard, cannot spend a single day without quarrelling : and why is it?   Thanks to our master, we are neither closely pent nor scantily fed.   Besides, it really is scandalous.   From the earliest times the dog has been the type of friendship ; yet you scarcely ever see any more friendship among dogs than among men."

"Let us make manifest an instance of it to our own times," says Polkan.

"Your paw !"

"There it is."

Straightway the new friends begin to caress and fondle each other.   They know not, in their raptures, to what to liken themselves.

"My Orestes !"

"My Pylades !"

"Away with all quarrels, all envy, all malice !"

Unluckily, at this moment the cook tosses a bone out of the kitchen.   Our new friends fling themselves upon it furiously. What has become of their harmonious alliance ? Orestes and

Pylades seize each other by the throat, so that their hair goes flying to the winds, and even torrents of water will scarcely separate them.

The world is full of such friendships. One would not be far wrong if one said of friends, as they are now-a-days, that they are almost all alike in respect to their friendship. To listen to them, you would imagine they were perfectly unanimous. But just throw them a bone; they will behave exactly like our dogs.*

* Kenevich says that this fable, which appeared in May, 1815, was suggested by the proceedings of the Congress of Vienna.

THE CUCKOO AND THE COCK.

"HOW proudly and sonorously you sing, my dear Cock!"

"But you, dear Cuckoo, my light, how smoothly flows your long-drawn-out note! There is no such singer in all the rest of our forest."

"To you, my dear gossip, I could listen for ever."

"And as for you, my beauty, I swear that, when you are silent, I scarcely know how to wait till you begin again. Where do you get such a voice from?—so clear, so soft, and so high! But no doubt you were always like that; not very large in stature, but in song—a regular nightingale."

"Thanks, gossip. As for you, I declare, on my conscience, you sing better than the birds in the garden of Eden. For a proof of this, I appeal to public opinion."

At this moment a Sparrow, which had overheard their conversation, said to them,

"You may go on praising one another till you are hoarse, my friends; but your music is utterly worthless."

Why was it that, not being afraid to sin, the Cuckoo praised the Cock? Simply because the Cock praised the Cuckoo.*

---

* This is said to allude to the perpetual interchange of compliments which used to take place between the editors of the " Northern Bee "—Grech and Bulgarine.

THE PEASANTS AND THE RIVER.

SOME Peasants, who had been driven out of all patience
by the ruin which the brooks and rivulets had brought
upon them by their overflowing, set out to seek redress from
the River into which those streams fell.   And, indeed, there
was much reason for denouncing them.   They had torn
away the seed from the newly-sown fields, they had over-
thrown and washed away mills, and it was impossible to
count the cattle they had drowned.   But the River flows so
gently, though indeed proudly: on its banks great cities
stand, and no one ever hears such tricks laid to its charge.
So, doubtless, it will put a check upon these streams.

Thus did the Peasants reason among themselves. But what happened? When they had drawn near to the banks of the River, and looked out upon its surface, they saw that its stream was bearing along half of their missing property. The Peasants, without beginning a fruitless complaint, only gazed on the waters for awhile. Then, after looking in each other's faces, and shaking their heads, they returned home; and as they went, they said,

"Why should we waste our time? You 'll never get any redress for what the children have stolen, so long as their parents go halves with them in the spoil."

[The best comment upon this fable is that supplied by Trutofsky's illustration of it. A number of peasants have come to lay before the district Ispravnik, or officer of rural police, a complaint against some of their petty oppressors. But, on arriving near the Ispravnik's house, they see that worthy standing in his verandah, benignantly smiling on the two men they have come to complain of, who are offering him a variety of presents, all of which the peasants recognise as having formerly belonged to themselves. Horrified at the sight, they are evidently about to retire without laying their case before such a judge.]

THE BAG.

AN empty Bag long lay neglected on the ground, in the corner of an antechamber, the lowest menials of the house
often using it as a mat to rub their shoes upon. But suddenly
our Bag was turned to honourable account, and filled full of
ducats. In an iron-bound coffer it now lies in security. Its
master caresses it with his own hand, and takes such care
of it that not a breath of wind is able to ruffle it; no fly dares
to light upon it. Besides this, the whole town becomes well
acquainted with the Bag. If a friend comes to visit its master,
he willingly begins to say pleasant things about the Bag.
Whenever it is opened, every one smiles sweetly upon it ; and
whoever sits down by its side is sure to pat it or stroke it
affectionately, seeing that it is universally respected. The
Bag begins to be puffed up, to make much of itself, to air its
cleverness. It begins to chatter and to give utterance to nonsense, discussing and criticising everything : " This is not so,"
and " That man is a fool," or " That affair will turn out badly."
Every one gives it his entire attention, listening with open
mouth, although it talks nonsense enough to make their ears
tingle. But, unfortunately, men have this weakness, that they
are sure to admire whatever a Bag says, so long as it is full
of ducats.

6—2

But did the Bag long enjoy honour?—did its reputation
for cleverness last, and was it long the object of endearment?
Only until its last ducat had been taken out of it: then it was
flung out of doors, and nothing more was ever heard of it.

[To this Bag Krilof compares many of the wealthy brandy-
tax farmers.* Some of them, he says, were once mere waiters
in petty taverns, but have now grown rich, and assumed airs
of importance. "A million is a great fact. Only, friends,
don't be too proud. Shall I whisper the truth to you? God
grant you may not get ruined! For, if you do, the same fate
will befall you that befell the Bag."]

---

* Contractors who farmed the tax on spirits, and made colossal fortunes, supplying
the peasants with the worst of liquors, and getting as much as they could out of them.
The whole system has now been altered, and this class of contractors no longer exists.

FORTUNE AND THE BEGGAR.

A WRETCHED Beggar, carrying a ragged old wallet, was creeping along from house to house; and, as he grumbled at his lot, he kept wondering that folks who lived in rich apartments, and were up to their throats in money and in the sweets of indulgence, should be always unsatisfied, however full their pockets might be, and that they should go so far as often to lose all they have, while unreasonably craving for, and laying their hands on, new riches. "Here, for instance," he says, "the former master of this house succeeded in trading prosperously, and made himself enormously rich by commerce. But then, instead of stopping, and hand-ing over his business to another, and spending the rest of his years in peace, he took to equipping ships for the sea in the spring. He expected to get mountains of gold ; but the ships were smashed, and his treasures were swallowed up by the waves. Now they all lie at the bottom of the sea, and he has found his riches melt away like those in dreams. Another man became one of the farmers of the spirit-tax, and so gained a million. That was a trifle : he wanted to double it. So he plunged up to his ears in speculations, and was utterly ruined. In short, instances of this are countless. And quite right too : a man should use discretion."

At this moment Fortune suddenly appeared to the Beggar, and said, " Listen ! I have long wished to help you. Here is a lot of ducats I have found. Hold out your wallet, and I will fill it with them ; but only on this condition :—All shall be gold that falls into the wallet ; but if any of it falls out of the wallet to the ground, it shall all become dust. Consider this well. I have warned you beforehand. I shall keep strictly to my compact. Your wallet is old ; don't overload it beyond its powers."

Our Beggar is almost too overjoyed to breathe. He scarcely feels the ground beneath his feet. He opens his wallet, and with generous hand a golden stream of ducats is poured into it. The wallet soon becomes rather heavy.

" Is that enough ?"

" Not yet."

" Isn't it cracking ?"

" Never fear."

" Consider, you 're quite a Crœsus."

" Just a little more ; just add a handful."

" There, it 's full. Take care : the wallet is going to burst."

" Just a little bit more."

But at that moment the wallet split ; the treasure fell through, and turned to dust ; and Fortune disappeared. The Beggar had nothing but his empty wallet, and remained as poor as before.

THE CUCKOO AND THE EAGLE.

THE Eagle promoted a Cuckoo to the rank of a Nightingale. The Cuckoo, proud of its new position, seated itself proudly on an aspen, and began to exhibit its musical talents. After a time, it looks round. All the birds are flying away, some laughing at it, others abusing it. Our Cuckoo grows angry, and hastens to the Eagle with a complaint against the birds.

"Have pity on me!" it says. "According to your command, I have been appointed Nightingale to these woods, and yet the birds dare to laugh at my singing."

"My friend," answers the Eagle, "I am a king, but I am not God. It is impossible for me to remedy the cause of your complaint. I can order a Cuckoo to be styled a Nightingale; but to make a Nightingale out of a Cuckoo—that I cannot do."

THE ASS.

A PEASANT had an Ass which seemed to behave itself so discreetly that he could not praise it too highly. But, in order that it might not get lost in the forest, our peasant tied a bell round its neck. On this our Ass, who had evidently heard a great deal of talk about decorations, became puffed up, began to grow proud and conceited, and looked upon itself as a very important gentleman. But its new rank proved ruinous to the Ass, poor thing!—a fact which may serve as a lesson for others besides asses. I ought to tell you beforehand that the Ass was never over-honest;

but until it got its bell everything went smoothly with it. If it made its way into a field of rye or oats, or into a garden, it ate what it wanted, and then got out again quietly. But now it is a very different story with him. Whenever our illustrious gentleman trespasses, the bell which now adorns his neck goes with him, and rings an incessant peal. Every-one looks out to see what it is. Here, one man, seizing a bludgeon, drives our poor beast out of his rye-field or his garden; and there, another, who owns a field of oats, no sooner hears the sound of the bell, than he catches up a stake, and begins thrashing the unfortunate animal's flanks. So that by the autumn our poor grandee is half dead : the Ass has nothing left but skin and bone.*

In the same way among men, also, rank proves injurious to rogues. As long as a rogue's position is humble, he is not remarked. But a lofty rank is, to a rogue, as it were a bell round his neck. Its noise is loud, and may be heard afar off.

---

* There is a good deal of resemblance between this Ass and the Dog in one of Æsop's fables.

THE LANDLORD AND THE MICE.

A CERTAIN Merchant built a magazine, in which he stored away his stock of edibles; and, in order that the mice should not damage them, he instituted a police of cats. And now the Merchant lives in peace. His stores are patrolled day and night, and all goes well. Unfortunately, an unexpected contingency occurs. One of the guardians proves himself a thief. Among cats, as with us (who knows it not?), the police are not faultless. But then, instead of detecting and punishing the thief, and sparing the honest servant, our landlord orders all his cats to be whipped. As soon as they hear this ingenious sentence, honest and guilty alike, they all run out of the house as quickly as possible: our landlord remains catless. This is just what the mice have been hoping and longing for. They enter the stores as soon as the cats have left, and in two or three weeks they contrive to eat up the whole of their contents.

[This fable, printed in 1811, probably alludes to the consequences of the wholesale punishment inflicted on the officials of the Commissariat and Victualling Departments during the war with France. They were disgraced in a body, and their uniforms were taken from them. The result was, that numbers of them retired from the service, rather than put up with such a slight. Krilof was interested in the matter; for the sister of one of his best friends was married to the General-Provision-Master.]

THE PEASANT AND THE SHEEP.

A PEASANT summoned a Sheep into court, charging
the poor thing with a criminal offence. The judge
was—the Fox. The case got into full swing immediately.
Plaintiff and defendant were equally adjured to state, point
by point, and without both speaking at once, how the affair
took place, and in what their proofs consisted.

Says the Peasant: "On such and such a day, I missed
two of my fowls early in the morning. Nothing was left of
them but bones and feathers. And no one had been in the
yard but the Sheep." Then the Sheep depones that it was
fast asleep all the night in question; and it calls all its
neighbours to testify that they had never known it guilty
either of theft or of any roguery; and, besides this, it states
that it never touches flesh-meat.

Here is the Fox's decision, word for word:

" The explanation of the Sheep cannot under any circum-
stances be accepted. For all rogues are notoriously clever
at concealing their real designs; and it appears manifest, on
due inquiry, that on the aforesaid night the Sheep was not
separated from the fowls; and fowls are exceedingly savoury,
and opportunity favoured it. Therefore I decide, according

to my conscience, that it is impossible that the Sheep could
have forborne to eat the fowls; and accordingly the Sheep
shall be put to death, and its carcase shall be given to the
court, and its fleece shall be taken by the plaintiff."

THE RAZORS.

A S I was travelling, one day, I fell in with an acquaintance, and we spent the night in the same bed-room. As soon as I awake next morning, what do I hear? My friend is evidently in trouble. The night before, we had both gone to bed merry and free from care; but now my friend is entirely changed: he groans, he sighs, he mutters words of complaining.

"What is the matter, my friend?" I cry. "You 're not ill, I hope."

"Oh, no," he replies; "but I 'm shaving."

"What! is that all?" I exclaim; and thereupon I get up

and look at him. The strange fellow is making faces at himself in the looking-glass, with tears in his eyes, and looking as agonized all the time as if he were expecting to be flayed alive. When I had at last discovered the cause of such sufferings, I say to him, " It 's no wonder, and it 's entirely your own fault that you are so much hurt. Just look at those things of yours. They are more like carving-knives than razors : as to shaving with them, that is impossible. All you can do is to scrape yourself painfully with them."

" I must allow, brother," he replies, " that the razors are excessively blunt ; how can I help knowing that ? I 'm not such a fool as all that. But I never use sharp ones, for fear of cutting myself."

" But I venture to assure you, my friend, that you will cut yourself much sooner with a blunt razor. With a sharp one you will shave yourself twice as safely ; only you must know how to use it properly."

Are there not many, though they would be ashamed to own it, who are afraid of clever people, and are more ready to have fools about them ?

—◆—

THE MONKEY AND THE MIRROR.

A MONKEY, which saw its image one day in a mirror, gave a Bear a slight push with its foot, and said, "Only look, my dear gossip, what a hideous creature that is! What grimaces it makes! How it skips about! I should hang myself from vexation if I were at all like that. But, if we must tell the truth, are there not in the number of our friends five or six such grimacers?"

"Why take the trouble to count up your friends? Would it not be better to take a look at yourself?" answered the Bear.

But Mishka's advice was only thrown away uselessly.

There are plenty of examples of this in the world. No one is ready to recognise himself in a satire. I remarked that only yesterday. We all know that Clement's hands are not clean. Every one charges Clement with taking bribes; but he shakes his head with secret horror when he thinks of Peter's unjust proceedings.

———◆———

THE ELEPHANT IN FAVOUR.

ONCE upon a time, the Elephant stood high in the good graces of the Lion. The forest immediately began to talk about the matter, and, as usual, many guesses were made as to the means by which the Elephant had gained such favour.

"It is no beauty," say the beasts to each other, "and it is not amusing. And what habits it has! what manners!"

Says the Fox, whisking about his brush, "If it had possessed such a bushy tail as mine, I should not have wondered."

"Or, sister," says the Bear, "if it had got into favour on account of claws, no one would have found the matter at all extraordinary; but it has no claws at all, as we all know well."

"Isn't it its tusks that have got it into favour?" thus the Ox broke in upon their conversation. "Haven't they, perhaps, been mistaken for horns?"

"Is it possible," said the Ass, shaking its ears, "that you don't know how it has succeeded in making itself liked, and in becoming distinguished? Why, I have guessed the reason. If it hadn't been distinguished for its long ears, it never would have got into favour."

THE WOLF AND THE MOUSE.

A GRISLY Wolf carried off a sheep from the fold into a retired nook in the forest—not from hospitality, one may well suppose. The glutton tore the skin off the poor sheep, and began devouring it so greedily that the bones cracked under its teeth. But, in spite of its rapacity, it could not eat it all up; so it set aside what remained over for supper, and then, lying down close by it, cuddled itself together at its ease, after the succulent repast.

But, see, the smell of the banquet has attracted its near neighbour, a young Mouse. Between the mossy tufts and hillocks it has crept, has seized a morsel of meat, and has run

off quickly to its home in a hollow tree. Perceiving the
theft, our Wolf begins to howl through the forest, crying,
"Police! Robbery! Stop thief! I'm ruined! I've been
robbed of everything I possessed!"

Just such an occurrence did I witness in the town. A thief
stole a watch from Clement, the judge, and the judge shouted
after the thief, " Police, police !"

THE PEASANT IN TROUBLE.

A THIEF crept into a Peasant's house one autumn night, and, betaking himself to the store-room,* rummaged the walls, the shelves, and the ceiling, and stole, without remorse, all he could lay his hands on. So that our Moujik, poor fellow, who had lain down a rich man, woke up so bereft of everything, that a beggar's sack seemed the only resource left him in the world. Heaven grant that none of us may ever know a similar waking! The Peasant weeps

* The *Kliet* is a sort of general store-room, serving the purposes of a larder, a clothes-press, &c.

and wails, and calls together his friends and relatives, his gossips, and all his neighbours.

"Can't you help me in my trouble?" he asks.

Then each begins to address the Peasant, and favours him with sage advice.

Says his gossip Karpich, "Ah, my light! you shouldn't have gone boasting to all the world that you were so rich."

Says his gossip Klimich, "In future, my dear gossip, you must take care to have the store-room close to the room you sleep in."

"Ah, brothers, you're all in the wrong," exclaims his neighbour Phocas. "The fault wasn't in the store-room being at a distance. What you must do is to keep some fierce dogs in your yard. Take whichever you please of my Jouchka's puppies. I would far rather cordially make a present of them to a good neighbour than drown them."

And thus, as far as words went, his loving friends and relatives gave him a thousand excellent pieces of advice, each according to his power; but when it came to deeds, not one of them would help the poor fellow.

THE SWORD-BLADE.

THE keen blade of a Sword, made of Damascus steel, which had been thrown aside on a heap of old iron, was sent to market with the other pieces of metal, and sold for a trifle to a Moujik. Now, a Moujik's ideas move in a narrow circle. He immediately set to work to turn the blade to account. Our Moujik fitted a handle to the blade, and began to strip with it lime trees, in the forest, of the bark he wanted for shoes, while at home he unceremoniously splintered fir chips with it. Sometimes, also, he would lop off twigs with it, or small branches for mending his wattled fences, or would shape stakes with it for his garden paling.

And the result was that, before the year was out, our blade was notched and rusted from one end to the other, and the children used to ride astride of it.   So one day a Hedgehog, which was lying under a bench in the cottage, close by the spot where the blade had been flung, said to it,

"Tell me, what do you think of this life of yours? If there is any truth in all the fine things that are said about Damascus steel, you surely must be ashamed of having to splinter fir chips, and square stakes, and of being turned, at last, into a plaything for children."

But the Sword-blade replied,

"In the hands of a warrior, I should have been a terror to the foe; but here my special faculties are of no avail. So in this house I am turned to base uses only. But am I free to choose my employment? No! Not I, but he, ought to be ashamed, who could not see for what I was fit to be employed."

THE RAIN-CLOUD.

A GREAT Cloud passed rapidly over a country which was parched by heat, but did not let fall a single drop to refresh it. Presently it poured a copious stream of rain into the sea, and then began boasting of its generosity in the hearing of a neighbouring Mountain. But the Mountain replied,

"What good have you done by such generosity? and how can one help being pained at seeing it? If you had poured your showers over the land, you would have saved a whole district from famine. But as to the sea, my friend, it has plenty of water already, without you adding to it."

[This fable is said to have been written on the occasion of certain grants of land made to the Governor of the Province of Pskof, during the prevalence of a terrible famine in that part of the country.]

THE WHISK.

GREAT honours were suddenly conferred upon a dirty Whisk.* It will not now any longer sweep the floors of kitchens ; for the master's caftans are handed over to it, the servants having, probably, got drunk. Well, our Whisk set to work vigorously. It was never tired of belabouring the master's clothes, and it thrashed the caftans like so much rye. Undoubtedly its industry was great ; only the misfortune was, that it was itself so dirty. Of what use, then, was all its toil ? The more it tried to clean anything, the dirtier did it make it.

Just as much harm is done when a fool interferes in what is out of his own line, and undertakes to correct the work of a man of learning.

---

* In Russian, a *Golik*. This is a provincial word, a native of the Province of Smolensk. The *Golik* is a bunch of bare twigs—*goly* meaning bare—greatly resembling our scholastic birch. The Russians make great use of it in their baths (see Dal's " Explanatory Lexicon of the living Great Russian Language," a work of the greatest value to every one who wishes to become really well acquainted with Russian literature.)

THE EAGLE AND THE SPIDER.

A^N EAGLE had soared above the clouds to the loftiest
peak of the Caucasus. There, on an ancient cedar
it settled, and admired the landscape visible at its feet. It
seemed as if the borders of the world could be seen from
thence. Here flowed rivers, winding across the plains ; there
stood woods and meadows, adorned with the full garb of
spring ; and, beyond, frowned the angry Caspian Sea, black
as a raven's wing.

"Praise be to thee, O Jove, that, as ruler of the world,
thou hast bestowed on me such powers of flight that I know
of no heights to me inaccessible !"—thus the Eagle addressed

Jupiter—"insomuch that I now look upon the beauties of the world from a point whither no other being has ever flown."

"What a boaster you are !" replies a Spider to it from a twig. "As I sit here, am I lower than you, comrade ?"

The Eagle looks up. Truly enough, the Spider is busy spinning its web about a twig overhead, just as if it wanted to shut out the sunlight from the Eagle.

"How did you get up to this height ?" asks the Eagle. "Even among the strongest of wing there are some who would not dare to trust themselves here. But you, weak and wingless, is it possible you can have crawled here ?"

"No; I didn't use that means of rising aloft."

"Well, then, how did you get here ?"

"Why, I just fastened myself on to you, and you brought me yourself from down below on your tail-feathers. But I know how to maintain my position here without your help, so I beg you will not assume such airs in my presence; for know that I——"

At this moment a gust of wind comes suddenly flying by, and whirls away the Spider again into the lowest depths.

THE MERCHANT.

"COME here, Andrew, my brother! Where have you got to? Come here, quickly, and admire your uncle's doings. Deal as I do, and you'll never suffer loss." Thus in his shop spoke a Merchant to his nephew. "You know that remnant of Polish cloth—the one we have had on our hands so long, because it was old, and damp, and rotten? Well, I've just passed it off for English. Here is a hundred-rouble note I have just this instant got for it. Heaven must have sent a fool this way."

"Just so, uncle, just so," replied the nephew; "only I'm

not quite sure as to which was the fool. Just look here; you 'll see you 've taken a forged note."

To cheat !—the Merchant cheated : there 's nothing wonderful in that. But if one looks around in the world a little higher than where the shops are, one sees that even there people go on in the self-same manner. Almost all of them are occupied in everything by the same calculation ; and that is, " How can one man best succeed in cheating another ? "

—◆—

THE PIG.

A PIG once made its way into the courtyard of a lordly mansion, sauntered at its will around the stables and the kitchen, wallowed in filth, bathed in slops, and then returned home from its visit a thorough pig.

"Well, Kavronya, what have you seen?" says the Swineherd to the Pig. "They do say that there is nothing but pearls and diamonds* in rich people's houses, and that there each thing is richer than the rest."

---

* One of Krilof's Russian critics, who has attacked this fable as being "low," finds

" I assure you they talk nonsense," grunted Kavronya. " I saw no riches at all—nothing but dirt and offal; and yet you may suppose I didn't spare my snout, for I dug up the whole of the back yard."

God forbid I should hurt any one by my comparison; but how can one help calling those critics Kavronyas who, in whatever they have to discuss, have the faculty of seeing only that which is bad?

---

fault with the two words *biser* and *jemchug*, used here by the Swineherd to describe something precious, saying that they both mean pearls. His remark holds good for the old Slavonic ; but in modern Russian *biser* means glass beads of various colours used for stringing, and *jemchug*, the real pearl.

THE FOX IN THE ICE.

VERY early one winter morning, during a hard frost, a Fox was drinking at an ice-hole, not far from the haunts of men. Meanwhile, whether by pure accident or from negligence doesn't much matter, the end of its tail got wet, and froze to the ice. No great harm was done; the Fox could easily remedy it. It had only to give a tolerably hard pull, and leave about a score of its hairs behind; then it could run away home quickly, before any one came. But how could it make up its mind to spoil its tail? Such a bushy tail as it was, so ample and golden! No; better wait a little. Surely, men are sleeping still. It's even possible that a thaw may, meanwhile, set in. In that case, it will be able to withdraw its tail easily from the ice-hole. So it waits: it goes on waiting, but its tail only freezes all the more. It looks round; the day is already beginning to dawn. People are stirring; voices are to be heard. Our poor Fox begins to rush about wildly—now this way, now that. But still it cannot free itself from the hole. Luckily, a Wolf comes running that way.

" Dear friend, gossip, father !" cries the Fox, " do save me I am all but lost !"

So the Wolf stopped, and set to work to rescue the Fox. Its method was a very simple one : it bit the tail of the Fox clean off. So our foolish friend went home tailless, but rejoicing that its skin was still on its back.

MIRON.

THERE lived in a certain city a rich man, named Miron.
Against this rich man arose complaints from his
neighbours on all sides. And the neighbours were so far
right that, although he had millions in his strong box, he
never gave a copeck to the poor.

But who is there who does not like to gain a good reputation? In order to give a different turn to the conversation
about him, our Miron made it publicly known among the
people, that in future he meant to give away food to the
needy every Saturday. And, indeed, any one who passed

his house, at the end of the week, could see that his gates were not closed.

"Poor fellow!" they think, "he will be utterly ruined." But of that there was no fear; for, every Saturday, he unchained a number of ferocious dogs, so that it was not a question with the poor who visited him of eating or of drinking, but simply of escaping, if Heaven willed it, with a whole skin.

In the meantime, Miron was looked upon as almost a saint. Every one said, "One can't sufficiently admire Miron; only it's a pity that he keeps such savage dogs, and that it's so difficult to get at him : otherwise, he is ready to give away all he has, even to the uttermost copeck."

It has often occurred to me to see how hard of access are the palaces of great people. But, of course, the fault is not due to the Mirons. It is always the dogs who are to blame.

THE WOLF AND THE FOX.

A FOX, which had feasted on fowls to satiety, and had set aside a good store of spare food, lay down under a haycock, one evening, to sleep. Suddenly it looks up, and sees a hungry Wolf dragging itself along to pay it a visit.

"This is terrible, gossip!" says the Wolf. "I cannot anywhere find even the smallest of bones to pick, and I am actually dying of hunger. The dogs are malicious, the shepherd won't sleep, and I have nothing left but to hang myself."

"Really?"

"Really and truly."

"My poor old gossip! But won't you take a little hay?

There is a whole haycock. I am delighted to oblige my friend."

But what its friend wanted was meat, not hay; and about its stock of provisions the Fox said never a word. So my grey-coated hero, though greatly caressed as to its ears by its gossip, had to go to bed supperless.

THE OWL AND THE ASS.

A BLIND Ass, which had undertaken a long journey, wandered from the road into a forest. As the night came on, our foolish fellow went so far into the thicket that it couldn't move either backwards or forwards; and even one who had eyes would have been unable to get out of that difficulty. But an Owl, by good luck, happened to be in the neighbourhood, and offered to act as a guide to the Ass. We all know how well Owls see at night. Hills, hillocks, ditches, precipices—all these our Owl distinguished as if it had been daylight, and, by daybreak, it had made its way with the Ass to the level road. Now, how could any one part with such a guide? So the Ass entreated the Owl not to desert it, and determined to visit the whole world in the Owl's company. Our Owl seated itself like a lord on the back of the Ass, and the two friends began to continue their journey. But did it prosper? No. The sun had scarcely begun to glow in the morning sky, when a greater than nocturnal darkness hid everything from the Owl's eyes. But our Owl is obstinate: it directs the Ass at random.

"Take care!" it cries. "We shall tumble into a pool, if we go to the right."

There was really no pool on the right ; but on the left there was even worse.

" Keep more to the left—another pace to the left !"

And—the Owl and the Ass fell into the ravine together.

THE MONKEY AND THE SPECTACLES.

A MONKEY became weak-sighted in old age. Now it had heard men say that this misfortune was one of no great importance; only one must provide oneself with glasses. So it gets half-a-dozen pairs of spectacles, turns them now this way and now that, puts them on the top of its head, applies them to its tail, smells them, licks them; still the spectacles have no effect at all on its sight.

"Good lack!" it cries, "what fools they be who listen to all the nonsense men utter! They 've told me nothing but lies about the spectacles. There isn't an atom of good in them."

Here the Monkey, in its vexation and annoyance, flung them down on a stone so violently that they were utterly broken to bits.

Unfortunately, men behave in the same way. However useful a thing may be, an ignorant man, who knows nothing about its value, is sure to speak ill of it, and, if he possesses any influence, he persecutes it too.

THE ELEPHANT AND THE PUG-DOG.

AN Elephant was being taken through the streets, probably as a sight. It is well known that Elephants are a wonder among us; so crowds of gaping idlers followed the Elephant. From some corner or other, a Pug-dog comes to meet him. It looks at the Elephant, and then begins to run at it, to bark, to squeal, to try to get at it, just as if it wanted to fight it.

"Neighbour, cease to bring shame on yourself," says Shafka * to it. "Are you capable of fighting an Elephant? Just see now, you are already hoarse; but it keeps straight on, and does not pay you the slightest attention."

"Aye, aye!" replies the Pug-dog, " that 's just what gives me courage. In this way, you see, without fighting at all, I may get reckoned among the greatest bullies. Just let the dogs say, 'Ah, look at Puggy! He must be strong, indeed, that 's clear, or he would never bark at an Elephant.'"

* Name given to a long-haired dog.

THE INDUSTRIOUS BEAR.

SEEING that a Peasant, who employed himself in making dugas,* disposed of them advantageously, a Bear determined to gain its living by the same business. The forest resounded with knocking and cracking, and the noise of the Bear's pranks could be heard a verst off. It destroyed a prodigious number of elms, birches, and hazels; but its labours did not lead to a good result. (For dugas are bent by dint of patience, and not in a moment.) So our Bear goes to the Peasant, and asks his advice, saying,

"Neighbour, what is the reason of this? I can break trees; but I haven't been able to bend one into a duga. Tell me, in what does the real secret of success consist?"

"In that," answered the Peasant, "of which, my friend, you haven't a bit—in patience."

---

* The *duga* is the wooden arch which, in a Russian cart or carriage, rises from the shafts above the horse's neck. When gaily painted and provided with bells, it is supposed to appeal to the animal's æsthetic tastes, and to encourage it to go on its way rejoicing. There are factories now in which *dugas* are made wholesale by steam-power.

THE FOX AS ARCHITECT.

A CERTAIN Lion was exceedingly fond of fowls, but they never throve with him. And that was no wonder. They lived utterly free from all restrictions; and so some of them were stolen, others disappeared of their own accord.

To remedy this unpleasantness and loss, the Lion determined to build a large poultry-yard, and so cunningly to design and arrange it, as entirely to keep out thieves, but to provide the fowls with plenty of space and all things needful.

Well, they inform the Lion that the Fox is a great hand at building, so the affair is entrusted to him. The building is begun and ended successfully, the Fox working at it with all conceivable industry and talent. The building is looked at and examined in detail. Truly, it is a work which cannot be too much admired. Everything is there which any one can possibly desire — food close at hand, perches inserted everywhere, refuges from cold and heat, and retired little places for the sitting hens. All honour and glory to our good Fox! A liberal reward is bestowed on him, and an order is given to transfer the fowls, without loss of time, to their new abode.

But is the change of any use? Not at all. It is true that

the building seems firm and massive, and the walls enclosing it lofty.   But yet the fowls daily become fewer and fewer. No one can imagine whence this evil springs.   But the Lion orders a watch to be set; and whom do they catch?   Why that villain, the Fox.   It is true that he had constructed the building so that no one else could break in and steal; but he had taken care to leave a little hole by which he could get into it himself.

FORTUNE'S VISIT.

AT the extremity of a town stood a wretched old house. In it lived three brothers, who could not get rich. Somehow, there was not a single thing that succeeded with them. Whatever any one of them took in hand was sure to prove unsuccessful: on all sides they met with hindrance and loss; and, according to them, it was all the fault of Fortune.

It happened that Fortune paid them a visit as she was passing by, and, touched by their great poverty, determined to do all she could to help them in everything they undertook, and to spend a whole summer with them. A whole summer !—a long time indeed.   Well, the poor fellows soon find their affairs assuming a different aspect.   One of them, although he was a poor hand at trading, gets a great profit now on everything he either buys or sells, utterly forgets that such a thing as loss exists, and rapidly becomes as rich as Crœsus.   The second enters the public service.   At another time he would have stuck fast among the copyists; but now he reaps successes on all sides.   Every time he gives a dinner, or pays a visit of ceremony, he gets either rank conferred upon him or a place given him.   See, he has an estate, a mansion in town, and a box in the country.

And now you will ask, what advantage did the third brother obtain ?   I suppose that Fortune really helped him also ?   Certainly; from his side she scarcely ever absented herself.   The third brother chased flies all the summer, and that with the most wonderful success.   I don't know whether he used to be clever at that sort of thing in former days, but during that summer his labour was never thrown away.   In whatever manner he moved his hand (thanks to Fortune), he never once missed his shot.

But see ! their guest, meanwhile, has brought her stay with the brothers to an end, and has set out on a long journey.   Two of the brothers have gained greatly.   One of them is rich; the other has got riches and rank besides. But the third brother curses his fate, inasmuch as malignant Fortune has left him nothing but a beggar's wallet.

THE LION, THE CHAMOIS, AND THE FOX.

A LION was chasing a Chamois along a valley. He had all but caught it, and with longing eyes was anticipating a certain and a satisfying repast. It seemed as if it were utterly impossible for the victim to escape; for a deep ravine appeared to bar the way for both the hunter and the hunted. But the nimble Chamois, gathering together all its strength, shot like an arrow from a bow across the chasm, and stood still on the rocky cliff on the other side. Our Lion pulled up short. But at that moment a friend of his happened to be near at hand. That friend was the Fox.

"What!" said he, "with your strength and agility, is it

possible that you will yield to a feeble Chamois? You have only to will, and you will be able to work wonders. Though the abyss be deep, yet, if you are only in earnest, I am certain you will clear it. Surely you can confide in my disinterested friendship. I would not expose your life to danger if I **were** not so well aware of your strength and dexterity."

The Lion's blood waxed hot, and began to boil in his veins. He flung himself with all his might into space. But he could not clear the chasm ; so down he tumbled headlong, and was killed by the fall. Then what did his dear friend do? He cautiously made his way down to the bottom of the ravine, and there, out in the open space and the free air, seeing that the Lion wanted neither flattery nor obedience now, he set to work to pay the last sad rites to his dead friend, and in a month picked his bones clean.

THE ORACLE.

IN a certain temple there was a wooden idol which began to utter prophetic answers, and to give wise counsels. Accordingly, it rejoiced in a very rich attire, being covered from top to toe with gold and silver; and was gorged with sacrifices, deafened by prayers, and choked with incense. Every one believed blindly in the Oracle.

All of a sudden—wonderful to relate !—the Oracle began to talk nonsense—took to answering incoherently and absurdly, so that, if any one consulted it about anything, whatever our Oracle said was a lie; so that every one wondered what had become of its prophetic faculty.   The fact was, that the idol was hollow, and the priests used to sit in it in order to reply to the laity; and so, as long as the priest was discreet, the idol did not talk nonsense; but when a fool took to sitting in it, the idol became a mere dummy.*

I have heard—can it be true?—that in days gone by there used to be judges who were renowned for ability—so long as they kept an able secretary.

---

* The word used is *bolvan*—the term irreverently applied by the common folk in Russia to most of their outdoor statues.

THE ASS AND THE PEASANT.

A PEASANT, who had hired an Ass for his garden during the summer, set it to drive away the impudent race of crows and of sparrows. The Ass was one of a most honest character, utterly unacquainted with either rapacity or theft. It never profited by a single leaf belonging to its master, and it would indeed be a sin to say that it connived at the proceedings of the birds. Still the Peasant got but little good out of his garden. The Ass, as it chased the birds with all its might, galloped across all the beds, backwards and forwards, in such a manner that it trod underfoot and trampled in pieces everything that grew in the garden.

Seeing then that all his pains were thrown away, the Peasant took a cudgel and revenged himself for his loss on the back of the Ass. "No wonder!" says every one; "serve the beast right! Was it for a creature of its parts to undertake such a business?"

But I say—though not with the intention of defending the Ass; it was certainly in fault, and it has already paid the penalty—surely he also was to blame who set the Ass to guard his garden.

THE SHEEP AND THE DOGS.

IN a certain flock of Sheep, it was resolved that the number of dogs should be increased, in order that the wolves might worry no more. What was the result? Why, the number increased so greatly that at last, truly enough, the Sheep were no longer annoyed by the wolves. But dogs, too, must live. So, first, they deprived the Sheep of their fleeces, and then they tore their skins off them, choosing them by lot. At last, only five or six of the Sheep remained, and those also the dogs ate up.

[In former days, whenever there was a difficulty about setting straight anything that had gone wrong in Russia, the only idea which suggested itself to the minds of the authorities was to increase the number of those officials who had to deal with the matter. But as these officials were miserably paid, they had to make a livelihood out of the people who were confided to their charge, and who, accordingly, fared no better than the sheep in the fable. Latterly, a different system has been introduced, and fewer but better paid officials are now employed.]

THE STRING OF CARTS.

A NUMBER of Carts, laden with pottery, were going along in a string, and had to descend a steep hill. Having left the others to wait a little on the top of the hill, the owner began very cautiously to lead down the first cart. The good horse which drew it almost supported the weight on its croup, not allowing it to roll down too fast. But a young Horse up on top took to blaming the poor animal for every step it made :

" Ah, praiseworthy animal ! how wonderful ! Just see, it crawls like a crab. See there, it has almost stumbled over a stone ! Look how awry, how askew, are its movements !

Ah! it's bolder now.   There's a jostle again !   Only here you ought to have gone a little more to the left.   Oh, what a donkey !   It would be all very well if this were night, or if it were going uphill.   But now it is going downhill, and by daylight.   One loses all patience while watching it.   Really it's a water-carrier you ought to be, if you have no sense in you.   But just look at us !—see how we will dash along. Never fear for us ; we wont lose a moment : we shall not so much carry our loads as whirl them down."

With these words, straining its back and inflating its chest, the young Horse sets its load in motion.   But no sooner does it commence the descent than the weight begins to press upon it heavily, the Cart to roll rapidly.   The Horse, urged on from behind, and thrust from side to side, dashes on splendidly at a gallop.   Over stones, across gullies, went the Cart amid shocks and boundings.   More to the left—still to the left, till at last the Cart and its load goes headlong into the ditch with a crash !   Farewell to the master's crockery.

[This fable alludes to the criticisms evoked by Kutuzof's unwillingness to precipitate matters in dealing with Napoleon. When he refused to fight under the walls of Moscow, the people began to clamour against him, as they had done against Barclay de Tolly ; and the younger officers under his command were especially indignant with him.   But Krilof took his part throughout.]

THE DIVERS.

A CERTAIN King, says Krilof,* could not make up his
mind as to whether knowledge and science produce
more good or harm. He consulted divers learned men on
the subject, but they could not solve the problem to his satisfaction. At last, one day, he met a venerable and remarkably intelligent hermit, to whom he confided his doubts, and
who favoured him with the following apologue:

"There was once a fisherman, in India, who lived on the
sea-coast. After a long life of poverty and privation, he died,
leaving three sons. They, seeing that their nets brought them
in but a scanty livelihood, and detesting their father's avoca-
tion, determined to make the sea yield them a richer recompense—not fish, but pearls. So, as they knew how to swim
and to dive, they gave themselves up to collecting that form
of tribute from it. But the three brothers met with very different kinds of success.

" The first, the laziest of the family, spent his time in saun-
tering along the shore. He had an objection to wetting even
so much as his feet, so he confined his expectations to picking

---

* I have thought it best to abridge the introduction, which is of inordinate length in
the original.

up such pearls as the waves might wash ashore at his feet. But the result of this laziness of his was that he scarcely made enough to keep him alive. As to the second, he used to dive, and find rich pearls at the bottom of the sea, never sparing any pains, and knowing how to choose those depths only which it lay within his power to sound.

"But the third brother, troubled by a craving after vast treasures, reasoned with himself as follows : 'It is true that there are pearls which one can find near the shore; but what treasures, apparently, might I not expect if I could only succeed in reaching the lowest depths of the open sea ! There, no doubt, lie heaps of countless riches—corals, pearls, and precious stones—all of which one might pick up and carry away at will.' Captivated by this ·idea, the foolish fellow straightway sought the open sea, chose the spot where the depths seemed blackest, and plunged into the abyss. But his recklessness cost him his life ; for the deep swallowed him down, and he never returned to the light of day.

"O King," continued the hermit, "no doubt we recognise in knowledge the source of many benefits. But those who seek it in an irreverent spirit may find in it an abyss in which they may perish, like the diver, but with this difference, that they may too often involve others in their own ruin."

THE TRIGAMIST.

A CERTAIN sinner, while his wife was still alive, married two other women. As soon as the news of this reached the King, who was a severe king, and disinclined to permit such scandals, he immediately ordered the polygamist to be tried for the offence, and ordained that such a punishment should be discovered for him as would terrify the whole people, so that no one should in future be capable of attempting so great a crime. "But if I see that his punishment is a light one," he added, "then I will hang all the judges around the judgment-seat."

This pleasantry is disagreeable to the judges. Fear bathes

them in a cold sweat.   For three whole days they deliberate
as to what punishment can be contrived for the culprit. Pun-
ishments are plentiful; but experience has proved that none
of them will deter people from sinning.   However, at last
Heaven inspired them. The criminal was brought into court
for the announcement of the judicial decision, by which they
unanimously decreed—

That he should live with all his three wives at once !

At such a decision the people were lost in astonishment,
and expected that the King would hang all the judges. But,
before the fifth day arrived, the Trigamist had hanged himself.   And the sentence produced such alarm that since that
time no man has committed trigamy in that country.

[This fable is not altogether original, being founded on a
misogenical pleasantry of great antiquity; but it is given as
a specimen of Krilof's terse style of story-telling.]

THE CUCKOO AND THE TURTLE-DOVE.

A CUCKOO sat on a bough, bitterly complaining.
"Why art thou so sad, dear friend?" sympathisingly cooed the Turtle-dove to her, from a neighbouring twig. "Is it because spring has passed away from us, and love with it; that the sun has sunk lower, and that we are nearer to the winter?"

"How can I help grieving, unhappy one that I am?" replies the Cuckoo: "thou shalt thyself be the judge. This spring my love was a happy one, and, after a while, I became a mother. But my offspring utterly refuse even to recognise me. Was it such a return that I expected from them? And how can I help being envious when I see how ducklings crowd around their mother—how chickens hasten to the hen when she calls to them. Just like an orphan I sit here, utterly alone, and know not what filial affection means."

"Poor thing!" says the Dove, "I pity you from my heart. As for me, though I know such things often occur, I should die outright if my dovelets did not love me. But tell me, have you already brought up your little ones? When did you find time to build a nest? I never saw you doing anything of the kind: you were always flying and fluttering about."

"Yes, indeed!" says the Cuckoo. "Pretty nonsense it would have been if I had spent such fine days in sitting on a nest! That would, indeed, have been the highest pitch of stupidity! I always laid my eggs in the nests of other birds."

"Then how can you expect your little ones to care for you?" says the Turtle-dove.

Fathers and mothers! let this fable read you a lesson. I have not written it as an excuse for undutiful children. Irreverence on their part, and want of love towards their parents, must always be a great fault. But, if they have grown up apart from you, and you have entrusted their education to hireling hands, have not you yourselves to blame, if in old age you obtain but little happiness from them?

THE LEAVES AND THE ROOTS.

ON a beautiful summer day, the Leaves on a tree whis-
pered softly to the zephyrs; and, as their shadow fell
upon the valley, thus did they speak, vaunting their luxuriant
verdure:

"Is it not true that we are the pride of the whole valley?
Is it not by us that this tree is rendered so bushy and wide-
spreading, so stately and majestic? What would it be without us? Yes, indeed; we may praise ourselves without
committing a sin! Do not we, by our cool shade, protect
the shepherd and the traveller from the heat? Do not we,
by our beauty, attract the shepherdess to dance here? From
among us, in the morning and the evening twilight, the nightingale sings; and as to you, zephyrs, you scarcely ever desert
us."

"You might add a word of thanks even to us," answered
a feeble voice from underground.

"Who is it that dares thus audaciously to call us to account? Who are you who are talking there?" the Leaves
began to lisp, noisily tossing on the tree.

"We are they," was the reply from down below, "who,
burrowing in darkness here, provide you with nourishment.

Is it possible that you do not recognise us? We are the roots of the tree on which you flourish. Go on rejoicing in your beauty: only remember there is this difference between us, that with the new spring a new foliage is born; but, if the roots perish, neither you nor the tree can survive."

[In the large illustrated edition of the fables, published four years ago, at St. Petersburg, this story is accompanied by one of Trutofsky's spirited drawings, which renders its meaning very clear. A couple of gentlemen and a lady, evidently belonging to the proprietor class, are sitting at their ease in a balcony; and down below, regarded by them with contemptuous wonder, stand half-a-dozen peasants, their clothes tattered, their figures emaciated, their faces worn with care. The fable was written in 1811, at a time when the question of the emancipation of the serfs was occupying considerable attention.]

THE WOLF AND THE CUCKOO.

"FAREWELL, neighbour!" said a Wolf to a Cuckoo. "In vain have I deluded myself with the idea of finding peace in this spot. Your people and dogs are all alike here—one worse than the other: even if you were an angel, you couldn't help quarrelling with them."

"And is my neighbour going far? and where is that people so pious that you think you will be able to live in harmony with them?"

"Oh! I am going right away to the forest of the happy Arcadia. There, it is said, they don't know what war is. The men are as mild as lambs, and the rivers flow with nothing but milk.   There, in a word, the Age of Gold is to be found.   Every one treats his neighbour like a brother ; and·it is even said that the dogs never bark there, much less bite. Tell me, dear friend, would it not be charming to find one-self, even in a dream, in so peaceful a land as that?   Fare-well ! Don't retain an unpleasant remembrance of me. There I shall really be able to live in harmony, in plenty, and in indulgence, and not, as here, have to be always on guard by day, and be deprived of one's quiet repose at night."

"A happy journey to you, dear neighbour," says the Cuckoo. "But, tell me, do you leave your teeth and your habits behind you, or do you take them with you ? "

"How could I possibly leave them behind me? What nonsense are you talking ? "

" Then, mark my words ! your skin won't remain long on your back there."

THE IMPIOUS.

IN the days of old there was a people, to the shame, be it said, of the nations of the earth, which became so hardened in heart, that it took up arms against the gods. Noisily, with countless banners displayed, the insurgent crowds overrun the plains, some armed with bows, others with slings. In order to kindle more fury among the people, the ringleaders, in the insolence of their hearts, declare that the tribunal of Heaven is harsh and foolish—that the gods either sleep or judge unreasonably—that the time has come to read them an unceremonious lesson—and that, as to the rest, it will not be difficult to hurl stones at the gods from the nearest hills, and to fill all Olympus with arrows.

Disquieted by the insolent blasphemies these fools uttered, all Olympus applied to Jupiter with the prayer that he would avert this evil. And even all the heavenly council was of opinion that, in order to confute the rebels, it would not be amiss to make manifest, at all events, a little miracle—a deluge or an earthquake, with thunder and lightning, or, perhaps, to crush them under a shower of stones.

"Let us wait a little," replied Jupiter; "for if they do not become quiet, but go on with their foolish violence, not fearing the immortals, they will be punished by their own deeds."

Then, with a roar, the banded rebels against the gods shot into the air a mass of arrows, a cloud of stones. But, laden with innumerable deaths, inevitable and terrible, their weapons fell back again upon their own heads.

THE FOX AND THE MARMOT.

"WHERE are you running so fast, gossip, without ever looking back?" a Marmot asked a Fox.

"Oh, my friend, my dear gossip, I have had a calumnious accusation brought against me, and I have been dismissed as an extortioner. You know, I was the judge of the poultry-yard. In that position I lost my health and my peace of mind. From the press of business, I never had time to get a comfortable meal, and at nights I could not sleep soundly. And now, in return for this, I have incurred the wrath of my employers, and all on account of a calumny. Only just think! Who in the world shall be without reproach, if calumnies are listened to? I an extortioner! Do they suppose I've gone out of my mind? Now, I appeal to you, have you ever seen that I took part in that wickedness? Think the matter over; reflect on it well."

"No, gossip, no; but I have often remarked that there was some down on your muzzle."

Many an official complains that he is forced to spend every rouble he has; and all the town knows that, originally, he had nothing, and that he got nothing with his wife. But

see ! little by little he builds a house; he buys an estate.
Now, in what manner can you reconcile his salary with his
expenditure ?   Although you can prove nothing against him
legally, yet you will not be committing a sin if you say,
"That fellow has down on his muzzle."

THE PEASANT AND THE ROBBER.

A PEASANT, who was beginning to stock his little farm, had bought a cow and a milk-pail at a fair, and was going quietly homewards by a lonely path through the forest, when he suddenly fell into the hands of a Robber. The Robber stripped him as bare as a lime tree.*

"Have mercy!" cried the Peasant. "I am utterly ruined. You have reduced me to beggary. For a whole year I have

---

* *i.e.*, Bare as a lime tree after it has been stripped of its bark, of which the peasants make shoes, baskets, &c.

worked to buy this dear little cow. I could scarcely bear to wait for this day to arrive."

" Very good," replied the Robber, touched by compassion; " don't cry out against me. After all, I shall not want to milk your cow, so I 'll give you back your milk-pail."

THE ANT.

A CERTAIN Ant had extraordinary strength, such as had never been heard of even in the days of old. It could even, as its trustworthy historian states, lift up two large grains of barley at once ! Besides this, it was also remarkable for wonderful courage. Whenever it saw a worm, it immediately stuck its claws into it, and it would even go alone against a spider. And so it acquired such a reputation on its ant-hill, that it became the sole subject of conversation.

Extravagant praise I consider poison ; but our ant was not of the same opinion : it delighted in it, measured it by its own conceit, and believed the whole of it. At length its head became so turned that it determined to exhibit itself to the neighbouring city, that it might acquire fame by showing off its strength there.

Perched on the top of a lofty cart-load of hay, having proudly made its way to the side of the moujik in charge, it enters the city in great state. But, alas ! what a blow to its pride ! It had imagined that the whole bazaar would run together to see it, as to a fire. But not a word is said about it, every one being absorbed in his own business. Our Ant seizes a leaf, and jerks it about, tumbles down, leaps up again. Still not a soul pays it any attention. At last, wearied with exerting itself, and holding itself proudly erect, it says, with vexation, to Barbos, the mastiff, lying beside its master's cart, "It must be confessed, mustn't it, that the people of your city have neither eyes nor brains? Can it really be true that no one remarks me, although I have been straining myself here for a whole hour? And yet I 'm sure that at home I am well known to the whole of the ant-hill."

And so it went back again, utterly crestfallen.

THE SLANDERER AND THE SNAKE.

ON the occasion of some triumphal procession in the realms below, the Snake and the Slanderer refused to yield each other precedence, and began a noisy quarrel as to which of the two had the best right to go first.

Now, in the infernal regions, as is well known, he takes precedence who has done most harm to his fellow-creatures. So in this hot and serious dispute, the Slanderer showed his tongue to the Snake; and the Snake boastingly talked to the Slanderer about its sting, hissed out that it was unable to put up with an affront, and strove hard to crawl past him. The Slanderer actually found himself being left behind. But Beelzebub could not allow this: he himself took the Slanderer's part, and drove the Snake back, saying,

"Although I recognise your merit, yet I justly assign precedence to him. You are excessively venomous, and dangerous in the extreme to everything which is near you; your sting is fatal, and you sting—which is no small merit— without provocation. But can you wound from afar, like the deadly tongue of the Slanderer, from whom there is no escape, even though mountains or oceans intervene? It is clear, then, that he is more deadly than you; so give place to him, and in future behave more quietly."

Since that time, Slanderers have been honoured more than Snakes in hell.

[In the first edition of this fable, which appeared in May, 1814, the triumphal procession was represented as taking place " on the birthday of Attila or Nero, or perhaps of Napoleon : I am afraid of stating which, for fear of making a mistake. But, after all, it 's no matter. In Satan's realms, such names are inscribed on a tablet, and great solemnities are appointed in their honour."

Krilof was " a good hater;" and he certainly did not like Napoleon.]

THE TWO DOGS.

BARBOS, the faithful yard-dog, who serves his master zealously, happens to see his old acquaintance Joujou, the curly lap-dog, seated at the window on a soft down cushion. Sidling fondly up to her, like a child to a parent, he all but weeps with emotion ; and there, under the window, he whines, wags his tail, and bounds about.

"What sort of a life do you lead now, Joujoutka, ever since the master took you into his mansion ? You remember, no doubt, we used often to suffer hunger out in the yard. What is your present service like ?"

"It would be a sin in me to murmur against my good fortune," answers Joujoutka. " My master cannot make enough of me. I live amidst riches and plenty, and I eat and drink off silver. I frolic with the master, and, if I get tired, I take my ease on carpets or on a soft couch. And how do you get on ?"

" I ?" replied Barbos, letting his tail dangle like a whip, and hanging his head. " I live as I used to do. I suffer from cold and hunger; and here, while guarding my master's house, I have to sleep at the foot of the wall, and I get drenched in the rain. And if I bark at the wrong time, I am whipped. But how did you, Joujou, who were so small and weak, get taken into favour, while I jump out of my skin to no purpose ? What is it you do ?"

" 'What is it you do ?' A pretty question to ask !" replied Joujou, mockingly. " I walk upon my hind legs."

[This fable is suspiciously like that by Izmailof, called " The Two Cats," which, in its turn, was adapted from Florian.]

THE STONE AND THE WORM.

"WHAT a fuss every one is making! How wanting in manners!" observed, with respect to a shower, a Stone which lay in a field. "Have the kindness to look. Every one is delighted with it. They have longed for it as if it were the best of guests; but what is it that it has done? It has come for a couple of hours or so—no more. But they should make a few inquiries about me. Why I have lain here for centuries. Modest and unassuming, I lie quietly where I am thrown. And yet I have never heard from a single person so much as a 'Thank you!' It is not without reason that the world gets reviled. I cannot see a grain of justice anywhere in it."

"Hold your tongue!" exclaimed a Worm. "This shower, brief as it has been, has abundantly watered the fields, which were being rendered sterile by the drought, and has revived the hopes of the farmer. But you contribute nothing to the ground but a useless weight."

Thus many a man will boast of having served the state for forty years; but as for being useful, he has never been a bit more so than the Stone.

THE KITE.

A KITE, which had been allowed to soar to the clouds, called out from on high to a Butterfly down below in the valley,

"I can assure you that I can scarcely make you out. Confess now that you feel envious when you watch my so lofty flight."

"Envious? No, indeed! You have no business to think so much of yourself. You fly high, it is true; but you are always tied by a string. Such a life, my friend, is very far removed from happiness. But I, though in truth but little exalted, fly wherever I wish. I should not like all my life long to have to conduce to some one else's foolish amusement."

# THE SQUIRREL IN SERVICE.

A SQUIRREL once served a Lion: I know not how, or in what capacity. But this much is certain, that the Squirrel's service found favour in the Lion's eyes; and to satisfy the Lion is, certainly, no light affair. In return for this, it was promised a whole waggon-load of nuts. Promised —yes; but, meanwhile, time continues to fly by. Our Squirrel often suffers hunger, and has tears in its eyes while grinning in the Lion's presence. When it looks round in the forest, its former comrades show themselves here and there high up among the trees. It looks at them till its eyes begin to blink; but they keep on always cracking nuts. Our Squirrel

11

takes a step towards the nut-bushes, looks at them—it can do no more.   At one time it is called away, at another it is even dragged off, on the Lion's service.

But see ! At last the Squirrel has grown old, and become tedious to the Lion.   It is time for it to retire.   They have granted the Squirrel its discharge, and they have actually given it the full load of nuts.   Excellent nuts—such as the world has never seen before.   All picked fruit—one as good as another ; a perfect marvel : only one thing is unlucky —the Squirrel has long ago lost all its teeth.

THE PEASANT AND THE AXE.

A MOUJIK, who was building a hut, got vexed with his Axe. The Axe became disagreeable to him ; the Moujik waxed wroth. The fact was, he himself hewed abominably ; but he lay all the blame on the Axe. Whatever happened, the Moujik found an excuse for scolding it.

"Good-for-nothing creature!" he cries, one day, "from this time forward I will never use you for anything but squaring stakes. Know that, with my cleverness and industry, and my dexterity to boot, I shall get on very well without you, and will cut with a common knife what another wouldn't be able to hew with an axe."

"It is my lot to work at whatever you lay before me," quietly replied the Axe to the angry rebuke, "and so your will, master, is sacred for me. I am ready to serve you in whatever way you please. Only reflect now, that you may not have to repent by-and-bye. You may blunt me on useless labour, if you will ; but you will certainly never be able to build huts with a knife."

THE SQUIRREL AND THE THRUSH.

A CROWD collected in a village, one holiday, under the windows of the seignorial mansion, looking, with open-mouthed wonder, at a Squirrel in a revolving cage. A Thrush also was wondering at it, perched on a neighbouring birch tree. The Squirrel ran so fast that his feet seemed to twinkle, and its bushy tail spread itself straight out.

"Dear old compatriot," asked the Thrush, "can you tell me what you are doing there?"

"Oh, dear friend, I have to work hard all day. I am, in fact, the courier of a great noble. So that I can never stop to eat, nor to drink, nor even to take breath;" and the Squirrel betook itself anew to running round in its wheel.

"Yes," said the Thrush, as it flew away, "I can see plainly enough that you are running; but, for all that, you are always there at the same window."

Look at some busybody or other. He worries himself; he rushes to and fro; every one wonders at him. It seems as if he were going to jump out of his skin; only, in spite of all that, he does not make any more progress than the Squirrel in the wheel.

THE ASS AND JUPITER.

WHEN Jupiter stocked the universe with the various tribes of animals, the Ass, among others, came into the world. But, either purposely or from an accident owing to the press of work at such a busy time, the Cloud-compeller made a sad mistake, and the Ass came out of its mould no larger than a squirrel. Scarcely any one ever took any notice of the Ass, although the Ass yielded to no one in pride. The Ass was much inclined towards boasting. But what was it to boast of? With such a puny stature, it was ashamed to show itself in the world. So our conceited Ass went to Jupiter, and began to pray for a larger stature.

"Have pity on me!" it cried: "how can I bear this misery? Lions, panthers, elephants, all obtain honour everywhere, and, from the highest to the lowest, every one goes on talking about them only. Why have you treated Asses so unkindly that they never obtain any honour, and not a word is ever spoken about them by any one? But, if I were only as big as a calf, I would lower the pride of the lions and panthers, and all the world would be talking about me."

Every day our Ass continued to sing this same song to Jupiter, and bothered him so that at last he granted its request, and the Ass became a big beast. But, besides this, it acquired such a savage voice that our long-eared Hercules dismayed the whole forest. " Whatever is that brute? What family does it belong to? It has very long teeth, anyhow, hasn't it? and no end of horns!" At last, nothing else was talked about besides the Ass.

But how did it all end? Before the year was out, every-one had discovered what the Ass really was. Our Ass became proverbial for stupidity, and, ever since that time, Asses have been beasts of burden.

Noble birth and high office are excellent things ; but how can they profit a man whose soul is ignoble?

THE CAT AND THE NIGHTINGALE.

A CAT, which had caught a Nightingale, stuck its claws
into the poor bird, and, pressing it lovingly, said,
"Dear Nightingale, my soul! I hear that you are everywhere renowned for song, and that you are considered equal
to the finest singers. My gossip, the Fox, tells me that your
voice is so sonorous and wonderful that, at the sound of your
entrancing songs, all the shepherds and shepherdesses go out
of their wits. I have greatly desired to hear you—don't
tremble so, and don't be obstinate, my dear: never fear; I
haven't the least wish to eat you. Only sing me something;
then I will give you your liberty, and release you to wander

through the woods and. forests.   I don't yield to you in love
for music, and I often purr myself to sleep."

Meanwhile our poor Nightingale scarcely breathed under
the Cat's claws.

"Well, why don't you begin?" continued the Cat.   "Sing
away, dear, however little it may be."

But our songster didn't sing; only uttered a shrill cry.

"What! is it with that you have entranced the forest?"
mockingly asked the Cat.   "Where is the clearness, the
strength, of which every one talks incessantly?   Such a
squeaking I 'm tired of hearing from my kittens.   No; I see
that you haven't the least skill in song.   Let 's see how you
will taste between my teeth."

And it ate up the poor singer, bones and all.

[This fable, which was published in the year 1824, is said
to be intended to depict the painful position which Russian
literature occupied at the time, with respect to the Censor-
ship.   During that period of reaction, the press was terribly
weighted; and it seemed that, at last, there would be no
subjects left of which it was not forbidden to take notice.
The censors acted just as they thought fit—altered manuscripts, prohibited books, and stopped the publication of
newspapers "till the editors should have knowledge enough
to conduct them properly."   It is a pleasure to compare the
position which the Russian press holds now, with that which
it occupied then.]

THE PEASANT AND THE HORSE.

A PEASANT was sowing oats one day. Seeing that, a young Horse began to reason about it, grumbling to itself.

"A pretty piece of work this, for which he brings such a lot of, oats here! And yet they say men are wiser than we are. Can anything possibly be more foolish or ridiculous than to plough up a whole field like this, in order to scatter one's oats over it afterwards to no purpose? Had he given them to me, or to the bay here, or had he even thought fit to fling them to the fowls, it would have all been more like business. Or even if he had hoarded them up, I should have recognised avarice in that. But to fling them uselessly away! No; that is sheer stupidity."

Meanwhile time passed; and in the autumn the oats were garnered, and the Peasant fed this very Horse on them.

Reader, there can be no doubt that you do not approve of the Horse's opinions. But, from the oldest times to our own days, has not man been equally audacious in criticising the designs of Providence, although, in his blind folly, he sees nothing of its means or ends?

THE GNAT AND THE SHEPHERD.

HAVING confided his sheep to the care of his dogs, a Shepherd went to sleep in the shade. Remarking that, a snake glided towards him from under the bushes, brandishing its forked tongue. The Shepherd would have passed away from the world, had not a Gnat taken pity on him, and stung him with all its might. Roused from his slumber, the Shepherd killed the snake. But first, while half awake and half asleep, he hit the Gnat such a slap that the poor thing was utterly done for.

There is no lack of examples of this. If the weak, even with the best intentions, try to open the eyes of the strong, you may expect that they will meet with the same fate as the Gnat.

A WOLF ran out of the forest into a village—not for a visit, but to save its life; for it trembled for its skin. The huntsmen and a pack of hounds were after it. It would fain have rushed in through the first gateway; but there was this unfortunate circumstance in its way, that all the gateways were closed. Our Wolf sees a Cat on a partition fence, and says, pleadingly,

"Vaska, my friend, tell me quickly which of the moujiks here is the kindest, so that I may hide myself from my evil foes? Listen to the cry of the dogs and the terrible sound of the horns! All that noise is actually made in chase of me!"

"Go quickly, and ask Stefan," says Vaska the Cat; "he is a very kind moujik."

"Quite true; only I have torn the skin off one of his sheep."

"Well, then, you can try Demian."

"I 'm afraid he 's angry with me, too. I carried off one of his kids."

"Run over there, then. Trofim lives there."

"Trofim! I should be afraid of even meeting him. Ever since the spring, he has been threatening me about a lamb."

"Dear me, that's bad! But perhaps Klim will protect you."

"Oh, Vaska, I have killed one of his calves."

"What do I hear, gossip? You've quarrelled with all the village," said Vaska to the Wolf. "What sort of protection can you hope for here? No; our moujiks are not so destitute of sense as to be willing to save you to their own hurt. And, really, you have only yourself to blame. What you have sown, that you must now reap."

THE CANNON AND THE SAILS.

A FIERCE quarrel arose on board a ship between its Cannon and its Sails. Poking their muzzles out of the port-holes, the Cannon thus murmured heavenward :

" O ye gods ! was ever such a thing seen, as that a set of trumpery linen fabrics should have the insolence to set up for being as useful as we are ? In the whole course of our laborious voyage, what have they done ? The moment a breeze begins to blow, they proudly swell out their breasts, carrying themselves above the waves as pompously as if they were really of great importance, but yet do nothing more than show off their airs. But, as for us, we thunder in battles. Is it not due to us that our ship rules the waves ? Do not we carry with us everywhere terror and death ? No ; we do not wish to live any longer with the Sails. We can do everything for ourselves without them. Fly, then, to our aid, mighty Boreas, and quickly tear them into rags."

Boreas heard, and, flying thither, breathed on the sea. Immediately the waters were overcast and turned black, a heavy cloud covered the sky, and the waves ran mountains high. Thunder deafened the ear ; lightning blinded the eye. Boreas roared, and tore the sails into shreds. When nothing was left of them, the tempest ceased. But what followed ?

Deprived of its sails, the ship became a sport to the winds and waves, and drifted about at sea like a log. And in the first encounter with a hostile vessel, which thundered terrible broadsides along its whole length, our ship, now unable to move, was soon riddled like a sieve, and went down to the bottom like a stone—Cannon and all.

Every state is strong when its elements are wisely balanced. By its Cannon it is terrible to its foes ; but its civil powers play the part of the Sails.

THE EAGLE AND THE BEE.

SEEING how a Bee was busying itself about a flower, an Eagle said to it, with disdain,

"How I pity thee, poor thing, with all thy toil and skill! All through the summer, thousands of thy fellows are moulding honeycomb in the hive. But who will afterwards separate and distinguish the results of thy labour? I must confess, I do not understand what pleasure thou canst take in it. To labour all one's life, and to have in view—what? Why, to die without having achieved distinction, exactly like all the rest. What a difference there is between us! When I spread my sounding pinions, and am borne along near the clouds, I am everywhere a cause of alarm. The birds do not dare to rise from the ground; the shepherds fear to repose beside their well-fed flocks; and the swift does, having seen me, will not venture out into the plains."

But the Bee replies,

"To thee be glory and honour! May Jupiter continue to pour on thee his bounteous gifts! I, however, born to work for the common good, do not seek to make my labour distinguished. But, when I look at our honeycombs, I am consoled by the thought that there are in them a few drops of my own honey."

Fortunate is he, the field of whose labour is conspicuous ! He gains added strength from the knowledge that the whole world witnesses his exploits.   But how deserving of respect is he who, in humble obscurity, hopes for neither fame nor honour in return for all his labour, for all his loss of rest —who is animated by this thought only, that he works for the common good !

THE LION.

WHEN the Lion became old and weak, his hard bed began to annoy him. It made his very bones ache; besides, it did not warm him. So he summons his nobles to his side, long-haired and shaggy wolves and bears, and says,

" Friends, to old bones like mine, my bed has now become intolerably hard. So find out some way, without oppressing either the poor or the rich, to collect fleeces for me, that I may not have to sleep on the bare stones."

" Most illustrious Lion!" answer the grandees, " who would think of grudging you his skin, not to speak of his fleece? And are there but few shaggy beasts among us here? As to stags, hinds, chamois, and goats, they scarcely pay any tribute at all. We will take their fleeces from them at once. They will not be any the worse for that; on the contrary, indeed, they will be all the lighter for it."

This very wise advice was immediately carried out. The Lion could not sufficiently praise the zeal of his friends. But in what had they shown themselves zealous? Only in this, that they caught the poor creatures, and sent them away completely shorn. But they themselves, though they were twice as hirsute, did not contribute so much as a single hair of their own; on the contrary, each of them who happened to be on the spot turned that tribute to good account, and provided himself with a mattress for the winter.

INDEX TO THE FABLES.

————o————

Dalziel Brothers, Camden Press, N.W.

The Book List

OF

STRAHAN AND COMPANY,

56, LUDGATE HILL, LONDON.

WORKS BY C. J. VAUGHAN, D.D.
VICAR OF DONCASTER.

Small 8vo. 2s. 6d.
Voices of the Prophets:
Or Faith, Prayer, and Holy Living.

Small 8vo. 2s. 6d.
Plain Words on Christian Living.

CONTENTS.

1. Sleep and Waking.
2. The Seat and Exit of Evil.
3. Temptation.
4. Conscience.
5. The Christian Use of Food.
6. The Christian Use of Society.
7. Domestic Service; (1) Masters and Servants.
8. Domestic Service; (2) Servants and Masters.
9. A Good Old Age.
10. Repentance and Forgiveness Once Needed.
11. Repentance and Forgiveness Occasionally Needed
12. Repentance and Forgiveness Daily Needed.
13. Address for a Harvest Home.
14. The Decisive Question.
15. The Marks of the Lord Jesus.
16. The Revelation of the Unseen.

Small 8vo. 2s. 6d.
Christ the Light of the World.

CONTENTS.

1. Why He Came.
2. The Lamp and the Light.
3. Nunc Dimittis.
4. Uses of Light.
5. A Man of Sorrows.
6. The Gospel of the Fall.
7. The Gospel of the Flood.
8. Christ the Lord of Nature.
9. Christ the Conqueror of Satan.
10. Christ the Destroyer of Death.
11. Christ the Sinner's Friend.
12. Cast Out and Found.

Small 8vo. 2s. 6d.
Characteristics of Christ's Teaching.
Drawn from the Sermon on the Mount.

CONTENTS.

1. Who are Happy? First, Second, and Third Answers.
2. Who are Happy? Fourth Answer.
3. Who are Happy? Fifth Answer.
4. Who are Happy? Sixth Answer.
5. Who are Happy? Seventh Answer.
6. Who are Happy? Eighth and Last Answer.
7. What are Christians? Two Answers.
8. Christ interprets the Law: Five Examples.
9. Christ warns us against Three Counterfeits.
10. Christ teaches us the Manner of Prayer.
11. Of the Candle of the Soul, which is a Single Intention.
12. Christ teaches us what we ought to Seek: Two Things.
13. Christ warns us against Judging.
14. Christ counsels Discrimination.
15. The Charter of Prayer.
16. Christ points out to us the Gate of Life.
17. Concluding Cautions.

WORKS BY HENRY ALFORD, D.D.
DEAN OF CANTERBURY.

Crown 8vo. and Small 8vo.
The New Testament.
A Revision of the Authorized Version. [*In the Press.*

Demy 8vo. 7*s.* 6*d.*
Essays and Addresses,
Chiefly on Church Subjects.

Crown 8vo. 3*s.* 6*d.* ; 12mo. 1*s.* 6*d.*
The Year of Prayer;
Being Family Prayers for the Christian Year.

Neat cloth, 9*d.*
The Week of Prayer;
An abridgment of "The Year of Prayer," intended for use
in Schools.

The Year of Praise;
Being Hymns with Tunes, for the Sundays and Holidays
of the Year.
There are Four Editions of this Book, viz.:—
I. Large Type, Imperial 16mo. price 3*s.* 6*d.* with Music. II. Small Type,
Crown 8vo. price 1*s.* 6*d.* with Music. III. Large Type, Small 8vo.
price 1*s.* without Music. IV. Small Type, Demy 32mo. price 6*d.*
without Music.

Small 8vo. 3*s.* 6*d.* each.
How to Study the New Testament.
Part I.—The Gospels and the Acts of the Apostles. Part II.—The Epistles
(Section I.) Part III.—The Epistles (Section II.), and the Apocalypse.

Small 8vo. 3*s.* 6*d.*
Eastertide Sermons.
Preached before the University of Cambridge.

Small 8vo. 5*s.*
The Queen's English.

Small 8vo. 3*s.* 6*d.*
Meditations :
In Advent, on Creation, on Providence.

Crown 8vo. 7*s.* 6*d.*
Letters from Abroad.

New and enlarged Edition, Crown 8vo. 5*s.*
Poetical Works.

WORKS BY DORA GREENWELL.

Crown 8vo. 6s.

Essays.

Contents :—
1. Our Single Women—2. Hardened in Good—3. Prayer—
4. Popular Religious Literature—5. Christianos ad Leones.

"Miss Greenwell's Essays are very graceful, and are written with a real knowledge of their subjects. The book is really a good one."—*Spectator*.

"We highly value all the Essays for their good sense, fine feeling, and hearty religiousness, and for the freshness and piquancy of their style. Together they form one of the most admirable pleas for, and defences of, Christian philanthropy which have lately issued from the press."—*Nonconformist*.

Enlarged Edition, crown 8vo. 6s.

Poems.

"Here is a poet as true as George Herbert or Henry Vaughan or our own Cowper. We advise our readers to possess the book, and get the joy and the surprise of so much real thought and feeling. It is a cardiphonia set to music."—*North British Review*.

"Miss Greenwell is specially endowed as a writer of sacred poetry; and it is the rarest realm of all, with the fewest competitors for its crown. She seems to us to be peculiarly fitted with natural gifts for entering into the chambers of the human heart, and to be spiritually endowed to walk there, with a brightening influence, cheering, soothing, exalting, with words of comfort and looks of love, as a kind of Florence Nightingale walking the hospital of ailing souls."—*Athenæum*.

"Amongst volumes of verse lately given to the world, none has truer and richer poetic qualities than this."—*Nonconformist*.

Small 8vo. 2s. 6d.

The Patience of Hope.

"This is the most thoughtful and suggestive book of our day."—*Witness*.

"A work of singular philosophic power, as well as poetic beauty."—*Family Treasury*.

"Our admiration of the searching, fearless speculation, the wonderful power of speaking clearly upon dark and all but unspeakable subjects, the rich outcome of 'thoughts that wander through eternity,' increases every time we take up this wonderful little book."—*North British Review*.

Small 8vo. 3s. 6d.

The Covenant of Life and Peace.

"The production of a thoughtful, cultivated Christian mind, setting forth, in great fulness and beauty, the present privileges of the believer."—*Baptist Magazine*.

Small 8vo. 3s. 6d.

Two Friends.

"We cannot read these pages without seeing that they are the production of a thoughtful and earnest mind."—*London Review*.

WORKS BY WILLIAM GILBERT.

2 vols. post 8vo. 21*s.*

The Wizard of the Mountain.

"Mr. Gilbert has here struck a new vein in which we hope he will continue to work. Many of the tales are perfectly fairy-like."—*Westminster Review.*

Crown 8vo. 6*s.*

Doctor Austin's Guests.

"More than any other writer of fiction that we could name, Mr. Gilbert possesses the power of investing an imaginary narrative with the character of a plain, unvarnished statement of facts. In reading his pages one seems to be listening to a person who is not broaching theories or communicating impressions, but simply registering, in a sober and straightforward manner, matters that have fallen under his observation or within his actual experience. His realism is the realism of Balzac and Defoe. We congratulate Mr. Gilbert on having made a decided advance in his art. This work is better, we think, than any of his previous ones."—*Saturday Review.*

Crown 8vo. Illustrated, 3*s.* 6*d.*

The Magic Mirror.

A Round of Tales for Old and Young.

"The stories are well told in the best style for children, and the little woodcuts to illustrate them have the merit of showing an unhackneyed mode of treatment."—*The Times.*

"This is such a book as Nathaniel Hawthorne alone could have written." —*New York Round Table.*

Crown 8vo. 6*s.*

De Profundis :

A Tale of the Social Deposits.

"Mr. Gilbert's novels do more to enlarge the field of actual experience than those of any other writer of the day. . . . Defoe and Mr. Gilbert alone of English novelists seem to give the ore of English life, while other novelists of equal power give only the extracted metal. . . . We think 'De Profundis' the most powerful of Mr. Gilbert's powerful stories." —*Spectator.*

"Mr. Gilbert has a dramatic faculty which many professed dramatists might well envy, and a purity of style which, in his department of literature, has only been surpassed by Defoe." —*Nonconformist.*

Square 16mo. Illustrated, 2*s.* 6*d.*

The Washerwoman's Foundling.

"A prettier tale for the Christmas season has not come under our notice amongst recently published stories. It is the most humorous prose poem we have read for many a day."— *Athenæum.*

WORKS BY EDWARD IRVING.

5 vols. demy 8vo. £3.

The Collected Writings of Edward Irving.

Edited by his Nephew, the Rev. G. CARLYLE, M.A.

*** *More than one-half of these Writings are now printed for the first time.*

"Edward Irving had the power of teaching the true sublime, and the English language can show no more magnificent specimens of religious eloquence than those that are contained in these Collected Writings."—*Times.*

"Irving, almost alone among recent men, lived his sermons and preached his life. His words, more than those of any other modern speaker, were 'life passed through the fire of thought.' He said out his inmost heart, and this it is that makes his writings read like a prolonged and ideal biography."—*The Saturday Review.*

"The greatest preacher the world has ever seen since apostolic times."—*Blackwood's Magazine.*

"Irving was the freest, brotherliest, bravest human soul mine ever came in contact with. I call him, on the whole, the best man I have ever, after trial enough, found in this world or now hope to find."—*Thomas Carlyle in "Fraser's Magazine."*

Post 8vo. 6s.

Miscellanies from the Collected Writings of Edward Irving.

"In preparing this portion of my lecture (that which had reference to Irving), I had occasion to consult the edition of his works published by Mr. Strahan of London, and also the selection which has been made of a volume of extracts from the larger work. I have no hesitation in giving the highest testimony in my power to the ability and tact shown in the latter piece of work. The volume of extracts will, I am confident, have the effect of making his countrymen appreciate the rare qualities of Irving as a preacher, in a manner the most pleasing and effective."—*Dean Ramsay, in his Lectures on "Preachers and Preaching," before the Philosophical Institution of Edinburgh.*

"It is by such a volume as this, we are inclined to think, that Irving will come to be widely known to general readers. There are passages of a purely theological character which, we think, display profound wisdom, and are models of clear, strong, living utterance. There are practical and ethical 'sayings,' that are as gold and rubies and diamonds. We entirely approve the principle of its compilation, and welcome it as fitted, in a very remarkable manner, to quicken genuine and deep religious feeling, and to impart earnestness and force to the religious life."—*Nonconformist.*

---

3 vols. demy 8vo. 15s. each.

Prophetical Writings of Edward Irving.

Vol. I. now ready.

WORKS BY THOMAS GUTHRIE, D.D.
EDITOR OF "THE SUNDAY MAGAZINE."

Crown 8vo. 3*s.* 6*d.*

Studies of Character from the Old Testament.

Crown 8vo. 3*s.* 6*d.*

Our Father's Business.

Crown 8vo. 3*s.* 6*d.*

Out of Harness.

Crown 8vo. 3*s.* 6*d.*

Man and the Gospel.

"In point of striking thought, as well as apposite and beautiful illustration, this work will stand comparison with any which bears its author's name. The subjects of which it treats are as varied as the are interesting, and belong to that class which, as Lord Bacon says, 'come home to men's business and bosoms.'"—*Edinburgh Courant.*

Crown 8vo. 3*s.* 6*d.*

The Parables

Read in the Light of the Present Day.

"No one can so fittingly explain the Parables of the New Testament as Dr. Guthrie. He is a master of imagery, who scarcely writes a sentence without a comparison, and who has, moreover, the no less essential qualities of clear spiritual insight and strong, shrewd sense."—*Freeman.*

Crown 8vo. 3*s.* 6*d.*

Speaking to the Heart.

"Dr. Guthrie never speaks without speaking to the heart; but these discourses bear with unwonted vividness the impress of his great emotional nature. They glow, they sparkle, they burn with intense feeling. We have seldom looked into a more fascinating book."—*English Churchman.*

32mo. 1*s.* 6*d.*

The Angels' Song.

32mo. 1*s.* 6*d.*

Early Piety.

WORKS BY ROBERT BUCHANAN.

Small 8vo. 5s.
London Poems.

"A series of life-like character-pictures. If Mr. Buchanan writes no more, he will have permanently enriched English literature by what he has already accomplished."—*British Quarterly Review.*

"There is something very graceful in every one of these dozen 'London Idyls,' and it is the grace of thorough completeness and proportion—the sound mind in the sound body—so far superior to any mere polish or trick of style. Several are exquisitely touching."—*Church and State Review.*

"We hardly know of any narrative poetry greater than is found in some of these sad and mourning lines. . . . These verses have been lived before they were written down."—*Athenæum.*

"No volume has appeared for many years in London which so certainly announces a poetic fame."—*Spectator.*

"As a poet combining simplicity with pathos and a wonderful talent for giving to his subjects the forms of reality and life Mr. Buchanan is unsurpassed. Among contemporaries and recent writers he is unequalled."—*Court Circular.*

"They are in their subject so pathetic—so repelling, one might almost say; in their realism so pre-Raphaelite; and yet in their poetic treatment so delicately and tenderly artistic ; that one cannot choose but wonder and admire, and be sad over them."—*Morning Star.*

Small 8vo. 5s.

Idyls and Legends of Inverburn.

"Mr. Buchanan is a man of original genius; such faculty as he has is independent, individual. And if we look closely into his poems we shall be struck with the fact that, although quite free from mannerism or eccentricity, which would call attention to any marked peculiarity isolating him from contemporaries, his thought and style are distinctively his own. He has none of the showy graces which make inconsiderate readers exclaim, 'How clever, how poetical !' While reading the poems you never think of the poet. It is only in the afterglow of emotion you think of him, and then

you know what rare power was needed to produce so genuine an effect."—Art. "Robert Buchanan," by G. H. Lewes, in the *Fortnightly Review.*

"One of the most charming volume. of poetic narrative that we know."—*Pall Mall Gazette.*

"We do not call to mind any volume of modern poetry so rich in tenderly told story, beautifully painted picture, and abundant, spontaneous music."—*Illustrated Times.*

"One who can write thus has a claim to be considered a true poet and master of hearts."—*Eclectic Review.*

Small 8vo. 5s.

Undertones.

"The offspring of a true poet's heart and brain, they are full of imagination, fancy, thought, and feeling; of subtle perception of beauty, and harmonious expression."—*Daily News.*

"Poetry, and of a noble kind."—*Athenæum.*

"Great intelligence, fine workman-

ship, and dramatic power almost unexampled in this half century."—*Illustrated Times.*

"It is life from within that in these pages invests the ancient myths with fresh meaning and beauty. Yet luxuriance of descriptive power there is too."—*Scotsman.*

WORKS BY ALEXANDER SMITH.

Crown 8vo. 6s. with Coloured Frontispiece.

A Summer in Skye.

"Mr. Smith has great command of language. Every page displays ingenious expressions, highly wrought comparisons, minute descriptions. 'A Summer in Skye' is to us very interesting indeed."—*Saturday Review*.

"With the exception of Mr. Ruskin and Mr. Kingsley, we should be puzzled where to go amongst living authors for better word-painting."—*Reader*.

"There are passages in the present volume which show the author's marvellous power of reproducing at will the magnificent effects of mountain scenery—passages in which a play of fancy and a true poetic insight strongly reinforce an illustration already presented with great facility of expression and rich colouring."—*Nonconformist*.

"Mr. Alexander Smith speaks of Boswell's Journal as 'delicious reading:' his own work, though after a very different fashion, affords delicious reading also. His egotism is never offensive; it is very often charming. If the traveller is sometimes lost in the essayist, who will not prefer an Elia to a Pennant?"—*Daily News*.

Crown 8vo. 3s. 6d.

Dreamthorp:

A Book of Essays written in the Country.

". . . A book to be read in the spirit of lazy leisure, to the sound of bubbling brooks and whispering woods. It is exquisitely printed, handy, handsome, and cheap."—*Athenæum*.

Crown 8vo. 6s.

Alfred Hagart's Household.

"The author paints with the most ordinary colours, but he has Opie's receipt for mixing them 'with brains.' It is his skill not only in selecting the most attractive and suggestive traits of character, but in expressing them in the most graceful and suggestive language, that gives unusual interest to 'Alfred Hagart's Household.' The author has the poet's power of translating tersely what he interprets from nature, of condensing vague feelings into tangible and graceful shape, and of mirroring by a simile what description would render inadequately. . . . Mr. Smith invests the simplest every-day characters and incidents with a freshness and grace which charm us."—*Pall Mall Gazette*.

"It is a sort of prose idyl, as dramatic in its details as 'Hermann and Dorotheas.'"—*Athenæum*.

"We want novelists with a touch of poetry in them. We want novelists whose love of the poetic will preserve them from sensational absurdities. Such a novelist we find in Mr. Smith."—*Press*.

"No one can read 'Alfred Hagart's Household' without a sense of keen enjoyment."—*Guardian*.

WORKS BY E. H. PLUMPTRE, M.A.
PROFESSOR OF DIVINITY, KING'S COLLEGE, LONDON.

2 Vols. post 8vo. 12*s.*

The Tragedies of Æschylus.

A New Translation, with a Biographical Essay, and an Appendix of Rhymed Choruses.

Popular Edition, crown 8vo. 7*s.* 6*d.*

The Tragedies of Sophocles :

A New Translation, with a Biographical Essay, and an Appendix of Rhymed Choruses.

"Let us say at once that Professor Plumptre has not only surpassed the previous translators of Sophocles, but has produced a work of singular merit, not less remarkable for its felicity than its fidelity ; a really readable and enjoyable version of the old plays."—*Pall Mall Gazette.*

Crown 8vo. 5*s.*

Lazarus, and other Poems.

" Professor Plumptre's freshness and originality of thought in treating familiar subjects give a great charm to what we may term his Biblical Idyls."—*Churchman.*

"The volume cannot fail to establish Mr. Plumptre's reputation as a devotional poet of a high order of merit."—*Morning Post.*

Crown 8vo. 5*s.*

Master and Scholar, and other Poems.

"The present volume will certainly add to Professor Plumptre's reputation. It is worthy to be put on the same shelf with Heber and his own favourite Keble."—*Westminster Review.*

Small 8vo. 6*s.*

Theology and Life.

"There is a degree of freshness and of originality about Mr. Plumptre's sermons which is wanting in a large majority of discourses. They contain the ring of true metal, and are of intrinsic value, independently of their suitableness to the immediate purpose of their delivery."—*Press.*

Demy 8vo. 12*s.*

Christ and Christendom ;
Being the Boyle Lectures for 1866.

"The Boyle Lectures for 1866 will stand not unworthily by the side of those produced by Professor Plumptre's most eminent predecessors. In them he displays, with rare force and constant readiness, all the resources of a ripe scholar, a keen critic, and an eloquent writer."—*Athenæum.*

8vo. sewed, 6*d.*

Sunday.

" A learned, comprehensive, and singularly candid and valuable treatise."—*Scotsman.*

WORKS BY HORACE BUSHNELL, D.D.

Crown 8vo. *7s. 6d.*

The Vicarious Sacrifice,

Grounded on Principles of Universal Obligation.

"This work is an important contribution to theological literature, whether we regard the amount of thought which it contains, the systematic nature of the treatise, or the practical effect of its teaching. No one can rise from its study without having his mind enlarged by its profound speculation, his devotion stirred by its piety, and his faith established on a broader basis of thought and knowledge."—*Guardian.*

Crown 8vo. *3s. 6d.*

Nature and the Supernatural,

As Together constituting the One System of God.

"It is a work of great ability, and full of thought which is at once true and ingenious."—*Edinburgh Review.*

Crown 8vo. *6s.*

Christ and His Salvation,

In Sermons variously related thereto.

"These sermons are distinguished from the ordinary discourses of the pulpit by being the product not merely of religious faith and feeling, but of religious genius."—*Atlantic Monthly.*

Crown 8vo. *3s. 6d.*

The New Life.

"We have here a Christian preacher dealing with some of the profoundest themes of Christian experience, with an insight into the working of the human soul, a grasp and breadth of thought, and a depth of experience, such as we have never seen equalled."—*Patriot.*

Crown 8vo. *3s. 6d.*

Christian Nurture,

Or the Godly Upbringing of Children.

"The thinking is original, vigorous, and suggestive. The book is one that cannot be read without profit and pleasure of no transient character."—*Montrose Standard.*

Crown 8vo. *3s. 6d.*

Work and Play.

"This book is a collection of papers on general subjects, treated in a religious spirit. To say that they are worthy of the writer is sufficient recommendation."—*Baptist Magazine.*

Limp cloth, *6d.*

The Character of Jesus.

WORKS BY JOHN DE LIEFDE.

2 Volumes, post 8vo. Illustrated, 22s.

Six Months among the Charities of Europe.

** This Work describes, among other representative Charities on the Continent, the large establishments devoted to the care of the Indigent, the Blind, the Fatherless, the Aged Poor, the Neglected Women and Children, and the Discharged Prisoners.

"The many thousands of English readers who are ready at home to take part in such works, and who would know, by faithful and pleasant report, what has been achieved elsewhere by the beneficent energies of earnest men and women, will find in this book a full body of the most pertinent information, full of encouragement and good suggestions."—*Examiner.*

"Mr. de Liefde's book is readable, interesting, stimulating. It shows how moral energy will overcome obstacles that seem enormous, how faith and enthusiasm move mountains."—*Fortnightly Review.*

"This book is excellent. It will be eagerly read by persons of practical benevolence. It shows how much can be done by determination and singleness of purpose to diminish the sum of human suffering, and to promote the happiness of mankind. Such a work cannot fail to be extensively appreciated."—*Daily News.*

Crown 8vo. Illustrated, 3s. 6d.

The Postman's Bag.

A Story-Book for Boys and Girls.

"This little volume is simple, artless, and Christian. We know several little children who are never weary of these stories, and we are sure that they can learn from them nothing but what is good."—*London Review.*

"Commend us to Mr. de Liefde for a pleasant story, whether in the parlour or on the printed page. He is himself a story-book, full of infectious humour, racy anecdote, youthful freshness, and warm-hearted religion. In this pretty little volume we do not get any of his more elaborate tales ; it is professedly a book 'for boys and girls,' and is made up of short stories and fables, the very things to win children's hearts."—*Patriot.*

Crown 8vo. 5s.

The Romance of Charity.

Being an Account of some Remarkable Institutions on the Continent.

"Mr. de Liefde may well call his volume 'The Romance of Charity,' for his collection of facts overpass fiction in strangeness. It is not very creditable that such vast works of Christian love should be absolutely unknown to, or unappreciated by, the approved leaders and principal advocates of our Church system in England. Some of the accounts given by Mr. de Liefde are most affecting and truly wonderful."—*The Dean of Canterbury in the "Contemporary Review."*

Crown 8vo.

Truth in Tales.

[*In the Press.*

WORKS BY GEORGE MAC DONALD LL.D.

Crown 8vo. *6s.*

.The Disciple, and other Poems.

"Year by year Mr. Mac Donald is winning his way to a high place among contemporary poets. Each new volume reveals fresh powers. The present volume contains, we think, the finest pieces he has written. It is both broader and manlier in tone and sentiment, and from an artistic point of view it shows an increased mastery of language and clearness of thought."—*Westminster Review.*

Popular Edition, crown 8vo. *3s. 6d.*

Unspoken Sermons.

"True and beautiful thought, musically and eloquently expressed."—*Pall Mall Gazette.*

"Readers will rejoice over these sermons as those who have gotten great spoil."—*Nonconformist.*

"In George Mac Donald's company the very air seems impregnated with love, purity, and tenderness. We seem to be under an Italian sky; and the harshness, whether of individual or national temperament, is wonderfully checked. A loving heart reveals to us the heart which is the fountain of love, and sends us away ashamed of our harsh and bitter feelings, and praying to be able to love more both Him who is Love and those who ought ever to be dear to us for His sake."—*Dr. Guthrie's "Sunday Magazine."*

Square 16mo. *2s. 6d.*, Illustrated by ARTHUR HUGHES.

Dealings with the Fairies.

"Mr. Mac Donald writes as though he had lived a long time in Fairy Land, and not from vague reports, but from notes taken on the spot."—*Spectator.*

"Mr. Hughes has illustrated these Fairy Tales with much skill; and the charming little volume, if it did not make us wish to be young again, did more, for while we were reading, so great was the magic of the Enchanter's Wand, we became young once more, and clapped our venerable hands over the tears of the Light Princess, and the groans of Mr. Thunderthump."—*British Quarterly Review.*

Popular Edition, crown 8vo. *6s.*

Annals of a Quiet Neighbourhood.

"It is as full of music as was Prospero's island ; rich in strains that take the ear captive and linger long upon it."—*Saturday Review.*

"A true and noble work."—*Daily News.*

"Whoever reads this story once will read it many times. It shows an almost supernatural insight into the workings of the human heart."—*Pall Mall Gazette.*

"This story is one that only a man of genius could have written."—*Examiner.*

WORKS BY THE AUTHOR OF "STUDIES FOR STORIES."

Crown 8vo. illustrated, *5s.*

A Sister's Bye-Hours.

"We put this book down with regret. We have said enough to show that it is brimful of true, warm affection, and that it is as faultless in language as it is simple in style."—*London Review.*

Crown 8vo. illustrated, *5s.*

Studies for Stories from Girls' Lives.

"Simple in style, warm with human affection, and written in faultless English, these five stories are studies for the artist, sermons for the thoughtful, and a rare source of delight for all who can find pleasure in really good works of prose fiction. . . . They are prose poems."—*Athenæum.*

"Each of these studies is a drama in itself illustrative of the operation of some particular passion—such as envy, misplaced ambition, sentimentalism, indolence, jealousy. In all of them the actors are young girls, and we cannot imagine a better book for young ladies."—*Pall Mall Gazette.*

"There could not be a better book to put into the hands of young ladies."—*Spectator.*

Square 16mo. illustrated, *3s. 6d.*

Stories Told to a Child.

"There is more real faculty in some of these brief tales than could be found by analysis in half the successful novels now published. One most pleasant thing about the book is, that though it is written for children by a brain capable of instructing the minds and ennobling the thoughts of grown people, there is no *coming down* to nursery intellects. The author's efforts are simply wide enough to embrace them, and catholic enough to be to them like the wholesome sunshine and wind. More than this it is not easy to say, but that may be said with entire confidence. Besides, there is a *goodness* about Miss Ingelow's stories, a vigour without rudeness, a piety without cant, a wholesome motherliness, which places them amongst the safest as well as the most intelligent things of the sort that we know of."—*Pall Mall Gazette.*

*** Each of the six stories in this book is issued separately, in neat cloth, price *6d.*

WORKS BY SARAH TYTLER.

Crown 8vo. *5s.*
Days of Yore.

"The concentrated power which we admire in 'Citoyenne Jacqueline' is precisely the kind of power to ensure an equal success to the author in 'Days of Yore.' No story in the book disappoints us : each has 'the virtue of a full draught in a few drops;' and in each there is the quintessence of such a novel as Thackeray might have written."—*Pall Mall Gazette.*

Crown 8vo. *6s.*
Citoyenne Jacqueline :
A Woman's Lot in the Great French Revolution.

"The author charms us immediately into keen interest in the scenes, and sympathy with the characters of her story, which shows a power of catching and reproducing to the life French piquancy and levity." — *Pall Mall Gazette.*

"'Citoyenne Jacqueline' is one of those rare books of which every sentence deserves to be read leisurely, and will repay the attention with pleasure."—*Guardian.*

"There is real genius in the book."—*Spectator.*

Crown 8vo. Illustrated, *5s.*
Papers for Thoughtful Girls.

"One of the most fascinating books we have ever seen for the rising youth of the fair sex. The whole volume is so lively and yet so serious, that we would disclaim all liking for the young lady who should not fall in love with it."—*Eclectic Review.*

Crown 8vo. *5s.*
The Diamond Rose :
A Life of Love and Duty.

"Story sweetly told. It is so full of character, it has such a depth of true human pathos about it, and—what in these days is no small merit—it is written in such an exquisitely perfect style, that we hope all our readers will procure it for themselves."—*Literary Churchman.*

Crown 8vo. *5s.*
Girlhood and Womanhood :
The Story of some Fortunes and Misfortunes.

"Every quality of merit which was conspicuous in 'Citoyenne Jacqueline' is apparent here also. The first tales in this volume give us some of the finest descriptions of scenery we have ever read, while the meditative mood into which Miss Tytler frequently falls in these eighteenth century reminiscences is very like the delightful chit-chat with which Thackeray indulged his readers so often."—*Spectator.*

Popular Edition, crown 8vo. Illustrated, *6s.*
The Huguenot Family in the English Village.

"'The Huguenot Family' ought to be called by a nobler name than 'a novel.' It claims analysis as an historical study of great value and beauty ; and as a story—as an example of character-painting, of the close and delicate representation of the gifts and graces, the struggles and triumphs of the human heart—it has few, if any, superiors. Grand'mère Dupuy is the finest creation of English fiction since Romola. The Parson's daughters would do no discredit to Oliver Goldsmith."—*Morning Post.*

WORKS BY NORMAN MACLEOD, D.D.

ONE OF HER MAJESTY'S CHAPLAINS.

Two Vols. crown 8vo. 16s.

The Starling.

A Scotch Story.

Popular Edition, Illustrated, crown 8vo. 6s.

Eastward:

Travels in Egypt, Palestine, and Syria.

[*In the Press.*

Sixteenth Thousand, crown 8vo. 3s. 6d.

The Earnest Student:

Being Memorials of John Mackintosh.

New Edition, Illustrated, crown 8vo. 3s. 6d.

The Old Lieutenant and His Son.

Ninth Thousand, crown 8vo. 3s. 6d.

Parish Papers.

Eleventh Thousand, Illustrated, square 8vo. 2s. 6d.

The Gold Thread:

A Story for the Young.

Thirty-fifth Thousand, sewed, 6d.

Wee Davie.

Second and Cheaper Edition, crown 8vo. 6s.

Reminiscences of a Highland Parish

Small 8vo. 2s. 6d.

Simple Truth spoken to Working People.

New Edition, in preparation,

The Home School.

WORKS OF FICTION.

3 vols. post 8vo. 31*s.* 6*d.*

The Man of Birth and the Woman of the People.

By MARIA SCHWARTZ.

"The story is undoubtedly clever, and is entirely free from the vulgar sensationalism which characterises too many of our modern works of fiction.

It is irresistibly enthralling and unexceptionally healthy in its tone."—*Nonconformist.*

3 vols. post 8vo. 31*s.* 6*d.*

Grace's Fortune.

"A thoroughly interesting novel. It avoids every approach to the sensational, and is written with very re-

markable ease and vigour."—*London Review.*

Post 8vo. 10*s.* 6*d.*

Lotta Schmidt,
And other Stories.

By ANTHONY TROLLOPE.

Post 8vo. 10*s.* 6*d.*

Arne :

A Sketch of Norwegian Peasant Life.

By BJORNSTJERNE BJORNSON.

Translated by AUGUSTA PLESNER and SUSAN RUGELEY-POWERS.

"The most charming love-story of the year."—*Illustrated Times.*
"Such fresh little bits of nature come to us rarely. They are green

spots in the arid waste of fiction. —*Athenæum.*
"It is, in fact, a fairy-book for men and women."—*Westminster Review*

Crown 8vo. 6*s.*

Wealth and Welfare.

By JEREMIAH GOTTHELF.

"For a long time we have not read a book in which the style was at once so fresh and individual without being

forced. This volume is a perfect little mine of shrewd observation." —*London Review.*

Crown 8vo. Illustrated, 5*s.*

A French Country Family.

By MADAME DE WITT, *née* GUIZOT.

Translated by the Author of "John Halifax, Gentleman."

"Madame de Witt is a charming painter of the natures and ways of well-nurtured children, and the Author of ' John Halifax, Gentleman,'

has done good service in giving us this English version of a book which will delight the inmates of our nurseries."
—*Athenæum.*

WORKS IN GENERAL LITERATURE.

Second Edition, crown 8vo. 5s.

On " Ecce Homo."

By the Right Hon. W. E. GLADSTONE.

" A curiously delicate essay on the method pursued in ' Ecce Homo,' the fine and complicated texture of which is in strange contrast with the bold doubts and bold dogmatisms of modern thought."—*Spectator*.

Crown 8vo. 6s.

Scripture Portraits, & other Miscellanies,

From the Published Writings of
A. P. STANLEY, D.D., Dean of Westminster.

Crown 8vo. 5s.

Essays from "Good Words."

By HENRY ROGERS, Author of "The Eclipse of Faith."

" Worthy of the ability of the author of 'The Eclipse of Faith.' "—*Spectator*.

Square 8vo. Illustrated, 12s.

La Belle France.

By BESSIE PARKES-BELLOC, Author of "Essays on Woman's Work," &c.

Small 8vo. 4s.

Essays on Woman's Work.

By BESSIE RAYNER PARKES.

" Every woman ought to read Miss Parkes' little volume on Woman's Work."—*Times*.

Small 8vo. 3s. 6d.

The Higher Education of Women.

By EMILY DAVIES.

"There is so much temperance, good sense, and originality in Miss Davies' treatment of the question, that it would be a most regretable thing if she failed to ensure a wide circle of readers."—*Westminster Review*.

Small 8vo. 5s.

Woman's Work in the Church.

Being Historical Notes on Deaconesses and Sisterhoods.

By JOHN MALCOLM LUDLOW.

"Of the importance of the subject of this book there can be no question, and Mr. Ludlow has brought to its discussion an intense sympathy, a large amount of information, and a calm, judicial spirit."—*British Quarterly Review*.

WORKS IN GENERAL LITERATURE.

Crown 8vo. *6s.*

Practical Essays on Education.

By THOMAS MARKBY, M.A.

Crown 8vo. *6s.*

Views and Opinions

By MATTHEW BROWNE.

"The work of a highly sensitive and cultivated mind. There is a rare and original vein of sportive humour running throughout its pages. . . . These are rare qualities; and the book in which they are displayed has few if any recent equals."—*Westminster Review.*

Post 8vo. *7s. 6d.*

Tangled Talk.

An Essayist's Holiday.

"'Tangled Talk' is the work of a true essayist. . . . It is a mosaic of suggestive bits; or, since mosaic is a false image, let us say it is a skein of bright and broken threads, every one of which may readily be woven into the reader's own thoughts, adding colour and strength to them for the future."—*Illustrated Times.*

Crown 8vo. *3s. 6d.*

Beginning Life.

By the Rev. PRINCIPAL TULLOCH.

"An excellent book for young men."—*Edinburgh Review.*

Small 8vo. Illustrated, *6s.* People's Edition, crown 8vo. Fancy Covers, *1s.*

The Autocrat of the Breakfast-table.

By OLIVER WENDELL HOLMES.

Crown 8vo. *3s. 6d.*

The Near and the Heavenly Horizons.

By the COUNTESS DE GASPARIN.

"This is a charming book. The Countess de Gasparin has the touch of genius which has the strange gift of speaking to everyone 'in their own tongue.'"—*Athenæum.*

Small 8vo. *5s.*

Human Sadness.

By the COUNTESS DE GASPARIN.

"There are times when the soul craves an utterance for its deeper longings. The Countess de Gasparin has given expression to these desires, and has done so in beautiful and affecting language."—*London Review.*

WORKS IN GENERAL LITERATURE.

Small 8vo. 3s. 6d.

Lights Through a Lattice.

By J. E. A. BROWN.

Square 8vo. 5s.

Gerhardt's Spiritual Songs.

Translated by JOHN KELLY.

Cloth extra, small 8vo. 4s. 6d.

The Hymns of Denmark.

Rendered into English by GILBERT TAIT.

Small 8vo. 5s.

Duchess Agnes, etc.

By ISA CRAIG.

"A book of verse which will certainly give Miss Craig a place among the sisterhood of living singers."—*Athenæum.*

Demy 8vo. 7s. 6d.

The Resources and Prospects of America.

Ascertained during a Visit to the States in the Autumn of 1865.

By Sir S. MORTON PETO, Bart. M.P.

"It deals entirely with the material and commercial capabilities of the country, and, as these are points on which it is almost impossible to take too sanguine a view, the book is likely to be equally acceptable on both sides of the Atlantic."—*Times,* April 12, 1866.

Small 8vo. Illustrated by Whymper, 3s. 6d.

The Regular Swiss Round.

In Three Trips.

By the Rev. HARRY JONES, M.A.

2 vols. demy 8vo. Illustrated, 21s.

Cosas de España:

Illustrative of Spain and the Spaniards as they are.

By Mrs. WM. PITT BYRNE, Author of "Flemish Interiors," &c.

"The best book we have yet seen on Spain."—*Daily News.*

Crown 8vo. 3s. 6d.

My Ministerial Experiences.

By the Rev. Dr. BUCHSEL, Berlin.

"This is an interesting volume. It contains very interesting accounts of the German Pietists, amongst whom Dr. Buchsel was constantly known, and who maintained the pure gospel in the midst of abounding Rationalism."—*Record.*

PHILOSOPHICAL & SCIENTIFIC WORKS.

Fifth and cheaper Edition, with Additions, Crown 8vo. *6s.*

The Reign of Law.

By the DUKE OF ARGYLL.

"This is a masterly book ... strong, sound, mature, able thought from its first page to its last."—*Spectator*.

Post 8vo. *6s.*

The Philosophy of the Conditioned:

Sir WILLIAM HAMILTON and JOHN STUART MILL.

By the Rev. H. L. MANSEL, D.D. Oxford.

"This volume is distinguished by the same clearness of style, cogency of argument, accuracy of information, and mastery of the subjects, which characterise all the other valuable productions of the author, and is on the points criticised a most successful as well as a most unsparing exposure of Mill's manifold errors."—*British Quarterly Review*.

Second Edition, with Additions, 2 vols. *14s.*

Henry Holbeach:

Student in Life and Philosophy.

A Narrative and a Discussion. With Letters to Mr. M. Arnold, Mr. Alexander Bain, Mr. T. Carlyle, Mr. A. Helps, Mr. G. H. Lewes, Rev. H. L. Mansel, Rev. F. D. Maurice, Mr. J. S. Mill, and Rev. Dr. J. H. Newman.

"The brave manner in which mere utilitarianism, materialism, positivism, and authority are grappled with, convinces the reader that he is in the hands of one who has read extensively and thought profoundly on all the terrible questions of the day."—*British Quarterly Review*.

Crown 8vo. *6s.*

Familiar Lectures on Scientific Subjects.

By Sir JOHN F. W. HERSCHEL, Bart.

"A book of most profound and romantic scientific charm."—*Spectator*.

Crown 8vo. Illustrated, *4s. 6d.*

God's Glory in the Heavens.

By W. LEITCH, D.D. late Principal of Queen's College, Canada.

With Thirty-six Illustrations, printed in Colours, Crown 8vo. *9s.*

A Year at the Shore.

By PHILIP HENRY GOSSE, F.R.S.

"A delicious book deliciously illustrated."—*Illustrated London News*.

Square 8vo. With Photographs and Plates, *12s.*

Our Inheritance in the Great Pyramid.

By Professor C. PIAZZI SMYTH, F.R.S.S.L. and E.

"We commend this work to all lovers of genuine goodness, of stubborn mathematics, and of adventurous theorizing."—*London Quarterly Review*.

Post 8vo. *8s.*

Outlines of Philosphy.

BY ALEXANDER VINET.

"This volume abounds in passages remarkable for deep thought and eloquent expression."—*Guardian*

BIOGRAPHICAL WORKS.

Popular Edition, 3 Vols. crown 8vo. *6s.* each.

Lives of Indian Officers,

Illustrative of the History of the Civil and Military Services of India.

By JOHN WILLIAM KAYE,

Author of "The History of the War in Afghanistan," &c. &c.

"We say at once that more admirably-written and interesting narratives are scarcely to be found in any literature. ... Mr. Kaye's 'Lives of Indian Officers' will take a high place among the standard books of England."—*Athenæum.*

Crown 8vo. *6s.*

Vignettes :

Twelve Biographical Sketches.

By BESSIE RAYNER PARKES.

"This is a very charming volume. It will make many acquainted with persons worthy of being known, who have hitherto been names and nothing more."—*British Quarterly Review.*

Crown 8vo. *3s. 6d.*   Pocket Edition, small 8vo. *2s.*

Praying and Working.

By the Rev. W. FLEMING STEVENSON.

"The story of the lives of noble and devoted men. ... This record of men's faith in God's help will be read with interest and sympathy, for it touches the electric chain with which we are darkly bound."—*Athenæum.*

Third and Cheaper Edition, Illustrated, crown 8vo. *6s.*

Memoirs of the Life and Philanthropic Labours of Andrew Reed, D.D.

Prepared from Autobiographic Sources by his Sons, ANDREW REED, B.A. and CHARLES REED, F.S.A.

"The sons of Andrew Reed have done a good work in publishing this memorial of their father."—*Athenæum.*

"A profoundly interesting piece of biography."—*Weekly Messenger.*

Crown 8vo. *3s. 6d.*

Story of the Lives of Carey, Marshman, and Ward.

By JOHN C. MARSHMAN.

THEOLOGICAL AND RELIGIOUS WORKS.

The Critical English Testament,

Being an Adaptation of Bengel's Gnomon, with numerous Notes, showing the Precise Results of Modern Criticism and Exegesis. Edited by Rev. W. L. BLACKLEY, M.A. and Rev. JAMES HAWES, M.A.

Complete in three volumes, averaging 750 pages, price 6s. each.

"A more valuable handbook for the Bible student could not have been supplied."—*British Quarterly Review.*

"The Editors of this valuable work have put before the English reader the results of the labours of more than twenty eminent commentators."—*Evangelical Magazine.*

Crown 8vo. 5s.

The Bible Student's Life of our Lord.

By Rev. SAMUEL J. ANDREWS.

"For most readers this book will be far more interesting than any other work on our Lord's earthly life."—*Contemporary Review.*

Crown 8vo. 3s. 6d.

The Foundations of our Faith.

By Professors AUBERLEN, GESS, and others.

"We know nothing that can compare with this work for completeness, wisdom, and power."—*Nonconformist.*

Small 8vo. 6s.

Personal Names in the Bible.

By the Rev. W. F. WILKINSON, M.A. Joint Editor of "Webster and Wilkinson's Greek Testament."

"This is a book for all who would wisely, justly, and carefully study the sacred volume."—*Homilist.*

Post 8vo. 8s.

Outlines of Theology.

By ALEXANDER VINET.

"This volume is of great merit and extreme interest. . . . Our readers will find in it a rich vein of vigorous thought, extremely suggestive, and always pervaded by a devout and reverent spirit."—*British Quarterly Review.*

New and Enlarged Edition. Crown 8vo. 5s.

The Christ of History.

By JOHN YOUNG, LL.D.

"The republication of Dr. Young's 'Christ of History,' with an appendix on Renan's 'Vie de Jésus,' is well timed. The argument is irresistible and unanswerable. We trust that this reappearance of a work of such great excellence, eloquence, and logical compactness will give fresh impetus to its study, and lead those who persist in approaching Christ on the strictly human side to cry, with the Apostle, 'My Lord and my God.'"—*British Quarterly Review.*

Post 8vo. 7s. 6d.

The Life and Light of Men.

By JOHN YOUNG, LL.D.

"The author's idea is beautifully worked out in this volume, which, like all Dr. Young's writings, is characterised by deep thought and the keenest appreciation of spiritual things."—*Spectator.*

THEOLOGICAL AND RELIGIOUS WORKS.

Crown 8vo. 5s.

Week-Day Sermons.

By R. W. DALE, M.A.

Crown 8vo. 3s. 6d.

Wind-wafted Seed.

Reprinted from " Good Words " and " The Sunday Magazine,"
Edited by NORMAN MACLEOD, D.D. and THOMAS GUTHRIE, D.D.

Crown 8vo. 3s. 6d.

The Treasure-book of Devotional Reading.

Edited by BENJAMIN ORME, M.A.

" The selections have been made with care, and will be prized not merely as something to be read in an idle hour, but to be pondered over." —*Literary Churchman.*
"This is a beautiful book, but its contents are even better than their accompaniment. Such a book, we feel, is not to be criticised save by one who should miss many of his favourite authors. But this is not likely to be the case."—*Spectator.*

Crown 8vo. 3s. 6d.

The Words of the Angels ;

Or, their Visits to the Earth, and the Messages they delivered.
By RUDOLPH STIER, D.D.

Crown 8vo. 6s.

The Prophet Jonah :

His Mission and Character Illustrated and Applied.
By the Rev. HUGH MARTIN, M.A.

" The work is both practical and expository, and will prove a valuable contribution to theological literature.
It is as well suited for general reading as for reference."—*London Review.*

Post 8vo. 7s. 6d.

Sermons and Expositions.

By the late JOHN ROBERTSON, D.D. Glasgow Cathedral.

" Dr. Robertson had not a superior among the Scottish clergy ; for manly grasp of mind, for pith and point in treating his subject, he had hardly an equal. Let it be added that a more genial, kindly, liberal-minded and honest man never walked this earth."
—*Fraser's Magazine.*

Demy 8vo. 7s. 6d.

Ecclesia Dei :

The Place and Functions of the Church in the Divine Order of the
Universe, and its Relations with the World.

"This is a very remarkable work, the execution of a grandly conceived theory. . . We fully expect to find that its intrinsic and literary excellence will soon force a way into public notoriety, and secure a due appreciation."—*John Bull.*

Crown 8vo. 2s. 6d.

Church Life :

Its Grounds and Obligations.
By the Author of "Ecclesia Dei."

THEOLOGICAL AND RELIGIOUS WORKS.

Crown 8vo. 2s. 6d.
On the Written Word.
By the Rev. J. Oswald Dykes.

Crown 8vo. 3s. 6d.
Prayers in the Congregation.
By Henry Ward Beecher, D.D.

Crown 8vo. 2s. 6d.
Life Thoughts.
By Henry Ward Beecher, D.D.

Crown 8vo. 3s. 6d.
Royal Truths.
By Henry Ward Beecher, D.D.

Crown 8vo. 3s. 6d.
Christian Believing and Living.
By F. D. Huntingdon, D.D.

Small 8vo. 5s.
The Restoration of the Jews :
The History, Principles, and Bearings of the Question.
By David Brown, D.D. Author of "The Second Advent."

Cloth antique, 1s. 6d.
The Pathway of Promise.

Small 8vo. 2s. 6d.
Able to Save ;
Or, Encouragement to Patient Waiting.
By the Author of "The Pathway of Promise."

Small 8vo. 2s. 6d.
The Throne of Grace.
By the Author of "The Pathway of Promise. '

Limp cloth, 8d.
Loving Counsel :
An Address to his Parishioners
By the Author of "The Pathway of Promise.

Crown 8vo. sewed, 1s.
Romanism and Rationalism as opposed to Pure Christianity.
By John Cairns, D.D.

THEOLOGICAL AND RELIGIOUS WORKS.

Cloth antique, 1s. 6d.

Personal Piety:

A Help to Christians to Walk worthy of their Calling.

Cloth antique, 1s. 6d.

The Sunday Evening Book for Family Reading.

Cloth antique, 1s. 6d.

Aids to Prayer.

Small 8vo. cloth antique, 3s. 6d.

Christian Companionship for Retired Hours.

Small 8vo. 3s. 6d.

Conversion.

By the Rev. ADOLPH SAPHIR.

Small 8vo. 1s. 6d.

The Higher Christian Life.

By the Rev. W. E. BOARDMAN.

Small 8vo. 1s. 6d.

The Way Home.

By the Rev. CHARLES BULLOCK.

Small 8vo. 1s.

Blind Bartimeus, and his Great Physician.

By the Rev. W. G. HOGE.

Limp cloth, 1s.

The Still Hour.

By AUSTIN PHELPS.

Small 8vo. 2s. 6d.

Man's Renewal.

By AUSTIN PHELPS, Author of "The Still Hour."

Small 8vo. 1s. 6d.

Prevailing Prayer.

With Introduction by NORMAN MACLEOD, D.D.

BOOKS FOR WORKING PEOPLE.

Seventy-second Thousand, crown 8vo. boards, 1*s*. 6*d*.
Better Days for Working People.
By WILLIAM G. BLAIKIE, D.D. F.R.S.E.

Fifth Thousand, crown 8vo. cloth, 3*s*. 6*d*.
Heads and Hands in the World of Labour.
By WILLIAM G. BLAIKIE, D.D. F.R.S.E.

Crown 8vo. boards, 1*s*. 6*d*.
Counsel and Cheer for the Battle of Life.
By WILLIAM G. BLAIKIE, D.D. F.R.S.E.

Crown 8vo. boards, 1*s*. 6*d*.
The Representation and Education of the People.
Lectures delivered at the Working Men's College.
By FREDERICK DENISON MAURICE, M.A.

Small 8vo. cloth, 2*s*. 6*d*.
Simple Truth spoken to Working People.
By NORMAN MACLEOD, D.D. One of Her Majesty's Chaplains.

Small 8vo. sewed, 6*d*.
Plain Words on Health.
Lay Sermons to Working People.
By JOHN BROWN, M.D.

Small crown 8vo. 2*s*. 6*d*.
Progress of the Working Classes from 1832 to 1867.
By J. M. LUDLOW and LLOYD JONES.

BOOKS FOR THE YOUNG.

Square 16mo. Illustrated, 1s. 6d.

The Will-o'-the-Wisps are in Town;

And other New Tales.
By Hans Christian Andersen.

Square 16mo. Illustrated, 2s. 6d.

Edwin's Fairing.

By Edward Monro, M.A.

Square 16mo. Illustrated, 2s. 6d.

Æsop's Fables.

Square 16mo. Illustrated, 2s. 6d.

Lilliput Levee:

Poems of Childhood, Child-fancy, and Child-like Moods.

Square 8vo. Illustrated, 3s. 6d.

Wordsworth's Poems for the Young.

Square 16mo. Illustrated, 3s. 6d.

Stories told to a Child,

By the Author of "Studies for Stories."

Square 16mo. Illustrated, 3s. 6d.

Poems Written for a Child.

By Two Friends.

Square 16mo. 1s. 6d.

Daily Devotions for Children.

Square 16mo. 1s. 6d.

Daily Meditations for Children.

FINE ART BOOKS.

Imperial 4to. cloth gilt, 21*s*.

Touches of Nature.

By Eminent Artists and Authors.

This Volume contains One Hundred Drawings on Wood, set in gold borders, and produced in the highest style of art, under the superintendence of Messrs. DALZIEL BROTHERS.

"This collection is one of the best that has ever appeared. It comprises drawings by Millais, Holman Hunt, Frederick Walker, Sandys, Wolf, Lawless, Du Maurier, Tenniel, Marcus Stone, Leitch, and half a dozen other men, more or less distinguished. Some of them are as good as can be found anywhere: Holman Hunt's drawing on p. 6 is an instance—a figure of a Jewish Reaper, which is beautiful beyond praise, a thing which demands and deserves contemplation as a masterly work of art. Besides Mr. Hunt, Mr. Millais and Mr. Walker are seen in this volume at their best, and so is Mr. Du Maurier."—*Pall Mall Gazette*.

"Millais's drawings here are all in his best style, and Mr. Holman Hunt's is perhaps the most remarkable in the collection. Mr. Sandys furnishes some very striking illustrations ; Mr. Wolf presents us with a collection of birds such as he alone can draw ; Mr. Linton a landscape, with one of those skies which he so much loves. We would gladly go on to specify others, but must content ourselves with briefly commending Mr. Small, Mr. Houghton, Mr. Walker, and especially Mr. Barnes ; and adding a word of deep regret for the loss of Mr. Paul Gray, whose pictures here show how true a lover of nature he was. But the chief value of the work is the testimony, which most certainly it bears, to the soundness and healthiness of English art in the present day. And it must be remembered that the illustrations were originally designed for 'Good Words,' the price of which is only 6*d*. ; but which fully deserves both its high reputation and wide circulation, by the spirit and good taste with which it is conducted."—*Westminster Review*.

Demy 4to. cloth gilt, 16*s*.

Millais's Illustrations.

A Collection of Drawings on Wood.

By JOHN EVERETT MILLAIS, R.A.

"Foremost among the Illustrated Books deserves to be named Mr. Millais's 'Collected Illustrations.' Mr. Millais has qualities as an artist with which few authors can dare a comparison. What these qualities are may be inferred from the fact that here are his best illustrations collected together, separate from the text to which they belonged. They are works of art that need no letterpress —no comment: they speak for themselves, and have an interest by themselves. They nearly all display extraordinary power, and some of them are in their way quite perfect."—*Times*.

"A collection of the choicest drawings that have appeared in 'Good Words' and other finely illustrated periodicals, has been collected into one handsome volume. By the phrase 'choicest drawings' we mean—nor do we think that the fitness of that phrase, so applied, will be for a moment questioned—the drawings of Mr. John Everett Millais. If anybody wishes to see how a great artist will condescend to learn the mechanism of any subordinate branch of art in which he is called upon to work, there is no better source of information on the point than this book affords. The wood-cutter has been met, and all his modes of effect have been considered by the painter, so that a perfect union of their forces has been gained, to the incalculable advantage of popular art."—*Daily Telegraph*.

" Good words are worth much and cost little."—HERBERT

Sixpence Monthly, Illustrated.

Good Words.

Edited by NORMAN MACLEOD, D.D.,

And Illustrated with Wood Engravings from designs by Millais, Holman Hunt, Keene, Walker, Wolf, Watson, and others.

The experiment has now been tried of establishing a Magazine which should reflect the every-day life of a good man—with its times of religious thought and devotional feeling, naturally passing into other times of healthy recreation, busy work, intellectual study, poetic joy, or sunny laughter ;—and its success has exceeded the most sanguine hopes of its projectors. "Good Words" was commenced ten years ago, and now enjoys a larger circulation than any other Monthly Magazine.—The following are among the Contributors to the Parts already published :—

Bishop Alexander.	J. M. Ludlow.
Dean Alford.	Miss Marsh.
Duke of Argyll.	Gerald Massey.
W. Lindsay Alexander, D.D.	Professor McCosh.
A. K. H. B. Author of "The Recreations of a Country Parson."	George MacDonald, LL.D.
Professor Ansted.	J. R. Macduff, D.D.
Rev. William Arnot.	Norman Macleod, D.D.
Rev. William Arthur, A.M.	Florence Nightingale.
Author of "John Halifax."	Mrs. Oliphant.
Rev. Thomas Binney.	Laurence Oliphant.
Professor J. S. Blackie.	F. Turner Palgrave.
Sir David Brewster, D.C.L.	Rev. J. J. Stewart Perowne, B.D.
John Brown, M.D.	Professor Lyon Playfair.
Robert Buchanan.	Professor J. L. Porter.
John Caird, D.D.	Adelaide A. Procter.
Isa Craig.	Rev. Charles Pritchard, F.R.S.
Rev. J. Ll. Davies.	Rev. W. Morley Punshon.
J. H. Merle D'Aubigné, D.D.	Rev. Professor Plumptre.
Principal Forbes.	Henry Rogers.
The Countess De Gasparin.	Samuel Smiles.
Mrs. Gatty.	Alexander Smith.
Archd. Geikie, F.G.S.	Professor C. Piazzi Smyth.
William Gilbert.	Dean Stanley.
The Right Hon. W. E. Gladstone.	W. Fleming Stevenson.
James Glaisher, F.R.S.	Bishop Tait.
Mrs. Margaret Maria Gordon.	Isaac Taylor.
P. H. Gosse, F.R.S.	Alfred Tennyson.
Dora Greenwell.	Sir W. Thomson.
Thomas Guthrie, D.D.	Rev. A. W. Thorold.
James Hamilton, D.D.	Anthony Trollope.
Sir John F. W. Herschel, Bart.	Rev. Principal Tulloch.
Jean Ingelow.	Sarah Tytler.
J. W. Kaye.	C. J. Vaughan, D.D.
Rev. Charles Kingsley.	Archbishop Whately.
Henry Kingsley.	Bishop Wilberforce.
Rev. Professor Lee.	Catherine Winkworth.

The Volumes of "Good Words" are Elegantly Bound in Mauve Cloth extra, and Full Gilt, price 7s. 6d. each.

*** Each Year's Issue forms a Complete Book.*

All the Volumes and Parts are in print, and may be had by order of any Bookseller.

Sevenpence Monthly, Illustrated.

The Sunday Magazine.

Edited by THOMAS GUTHRIE, D.D.

And illustrated with Wood Engravings from Designs by Watson, Houghton, Du Maurier, E. Hughes, Small, Pinwell, and others.

(From Note by the Editor.)

While aiming to bring the Bible into relation to common life, the "Sunday Magazine" seeks to express the devoutest thoughts of worship. Theology and the story of the Church; missions and missionaries; illustrations of God's glory in His works, and God's care in His providence; homilies on daily duties; and tales and sketches of character, all find a place. Human life has many relations, Christian experience many shades, the truth many sides : this Magazine addresses itself to each.

The Four Volumes of the "Sunday Magazine" already published contain the following Serial Works, among many others:—

ANNALS OF A QUIET NEIGHBOURHOOD. By George MacDonald, LL.D.

OLD TESTAMENT CHARACTERS. By Thomas Guthrie, D.D.

PICTURES FROM CHURCH HISTORY. By Islay Burns, D.D.

THE SEABOARD PARISH. By the Author of "Annals of a Quiet Neighbourhood."

HEROES AND MARTYRS OF THE REFORMATION IN ITALY. By W. L. Alexander, D.D.

IN THE LIFE OF OUR LORD. By William Hanna, D.D.

HOW TO STUDY THE NEW TESTAMENT. By Henry Alford, D.D. Dean of Canterbury.

OCCUPATIONS OF A RETIRED LIFE. By Edward Garrett.

THE CHRISTIAN LIFE IN VERSE.

THE METAPHORS OF ST. PAUL. By J. S. Howson, D.D.

THE HUGUENOT FAMILY IN THE ENGLISH VILLAGE. By Sarah Tytler.

THE SEVEN CONSCIENCES. By John De Liefde.

LUTHER THE SINGER. By George MacDonald, LL.D.

And numerous contributions by the Duke of Argyll; Dean Ramsay: Canon Girdlestone; C. J. Vaughan, D.D.; Norman Macleod, D.D.; J. C. Ryle, D.D.; Alexander Raleigh, D.D.; A. Thomson, D.D.; J. R. Macduff, D.D.; J. C. Miller, D.D.; Professor Plumptre; Professor A. H. Charteris; H. B. Tristram, LL.D.; Revs. W. F. Stevenson, A. W. Thorold, W. Arnot, Newman Hall, R. W. Dale, Hugh Macmillan, Henry Allon, Samuel Cox, J. Oswald Dykes, the late Professor Miller, James Hamilton, D.D., and Rev. Andrew Crichton, A.K.H.B.; Misses Isa Craig, Jean Ingelow, Dora Greenwell, Isabella Fyvie, and Sarah Tytler; Mrs. Sewell; and others.

The Yearly Volumes of the "Sunday Magazine" are Handsomely Bound in cloth extra, and Full Gilt, 8s. 6d. each.

**** Each Year's Issue forms a Complete Book.*

All the Volumes and Parts are in print, and may be had by order of any Bookseller.